MUMFORD & SONS

SIGH NO MORE

W9-ATE-715

Contents

ISBN 978-1-61774-108-1

HAL•LEONARD®
CORPORATION

7777 W. BLUEMOUND RD. P.O. BOX 13819 MILWAUKEE, WI 53213

Visit Hal Leonard Online at
www.halleonard.com

SIGH NO MORE

Words and Music by
MUMFORD & SONS

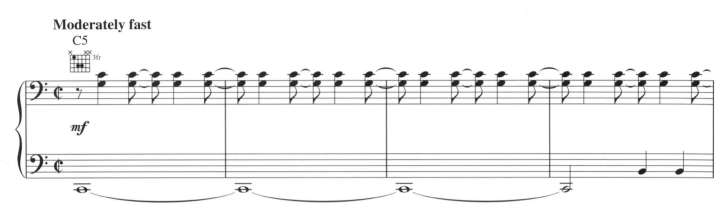

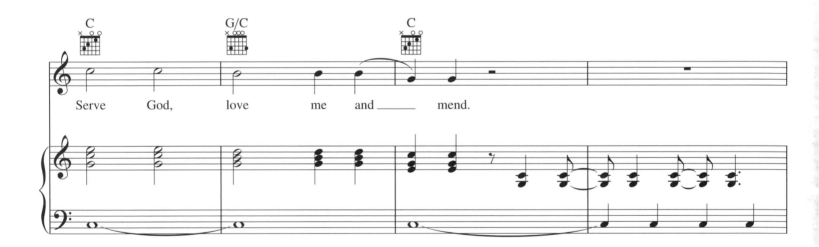

Serve God, love me and ____ mend.

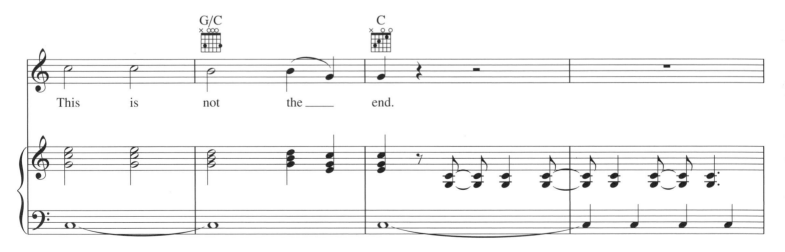

This is not the ____ end.

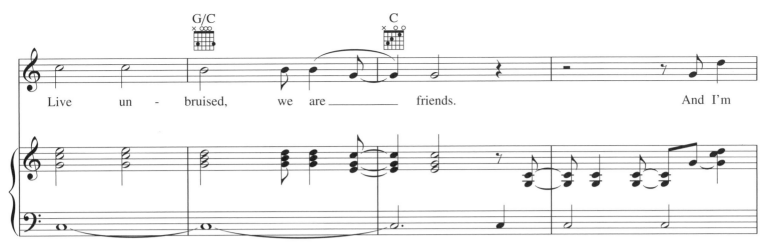

Live un - bruised, we are _____ friends. And I'm

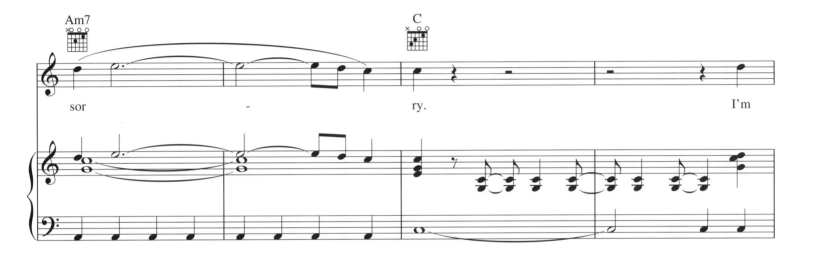

sor - ry. I'm

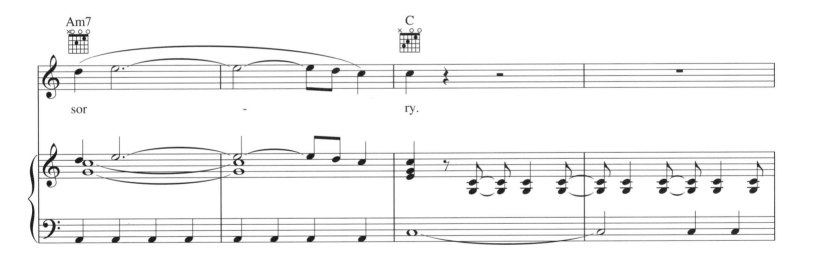

sor - ry. And I'm

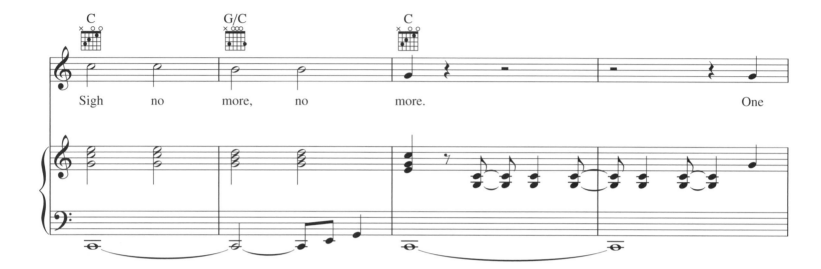

Sigh no more, no more. One

foot in sea, one on _____ shore. My

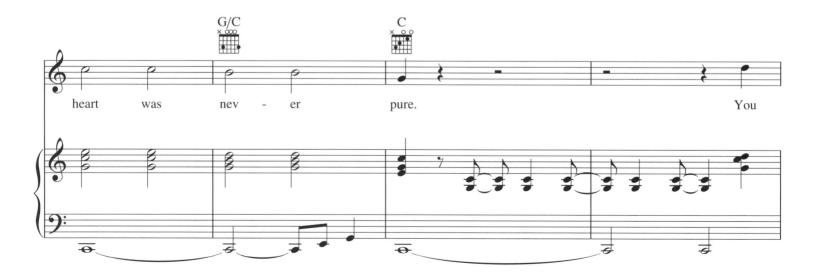

heart was nev - er pure. You

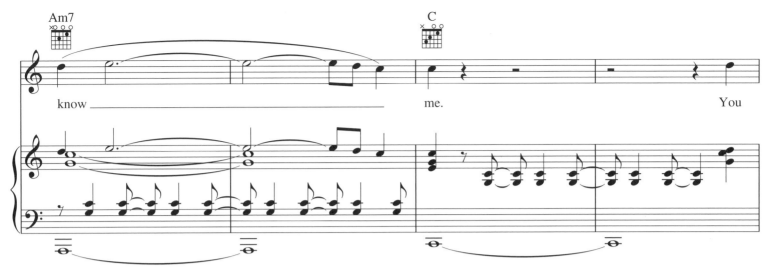

know _____ me. You

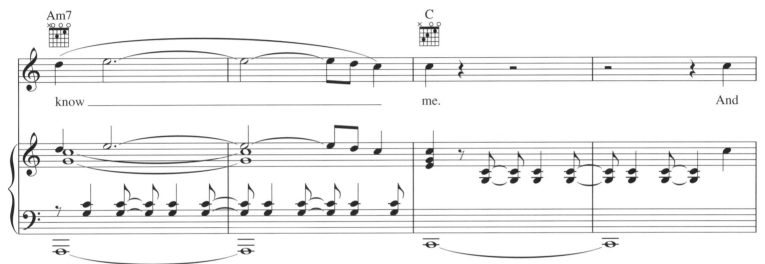

know _____ me. And

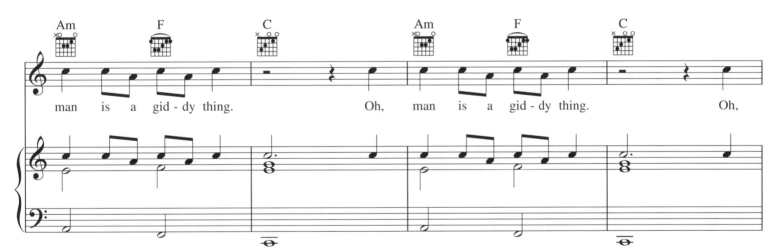

man is a gid-dy thing. Oh, man is a gid-dy thing. Oh,

man is a gid-dy thing. Oh, man is a gid-dy thing.

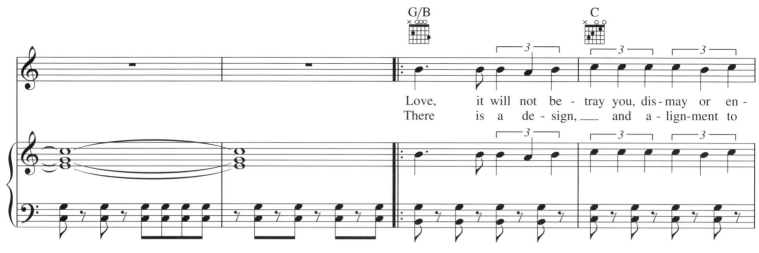

Love, it will not be - tray you, dis - may or en -
There is a de - sign, ___ and a - lign - ment to

slave you. __ It will set ___ you free. __ Be more like the ___ man you were made __
cry, ___ of my heart ___ to see ___ the beau - ty of ___ love as it was made __

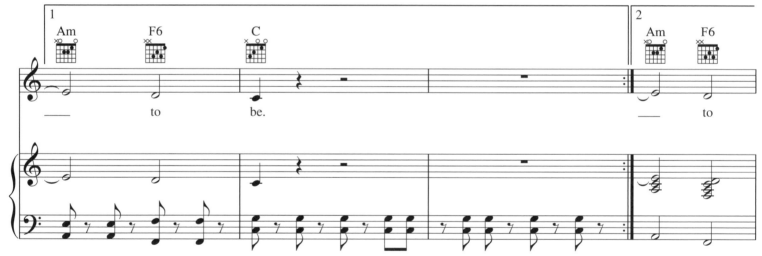

___ to be. ___ to

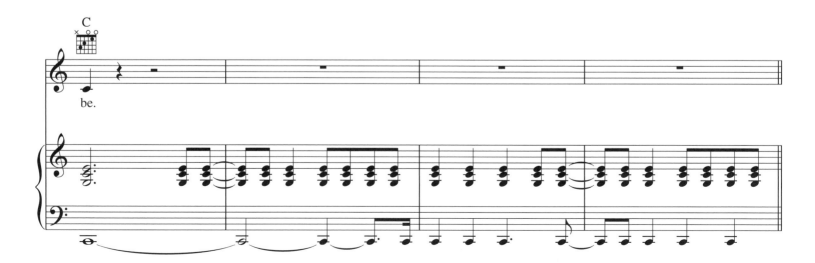

be.

(1.,3.) Love, it will not be - tray you, dis - may or en - slave you. It will set ___ you
(2.,4.) There is a de - sign, ___ and a - lign - ment to cry, ___ of my heart ___ to

free. ___ Be more like the ___ man you were made ___ to be.
see ___ the beau - ty of ___ love as it was made ___

___ to be.

D.S. al Coda
(with repeat)

CODA

___ to be.

THE CAVE

Words and Music by
MUMFORD & SONS

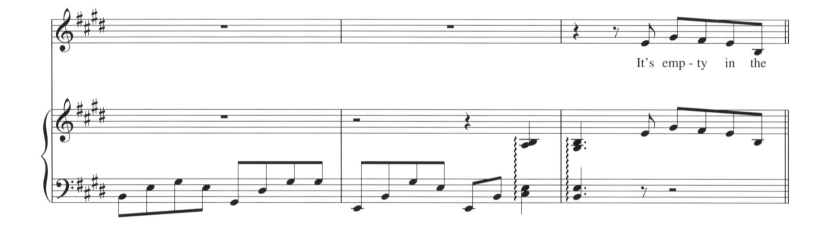

It's emp-ty in the

val - ley of your heart.   The sun, it ris - es slow - ly as you
fruit for you to eat,   you can - ni - bal, you meat - eat - er, you
things to fill my time.   You take what is yours and I'll take
post and block my ears.   I can see wid-ows and or - phans through my

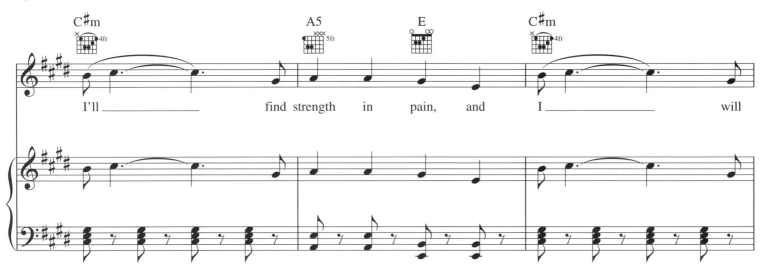

I'll _____ find strength in pain, and I _____ will

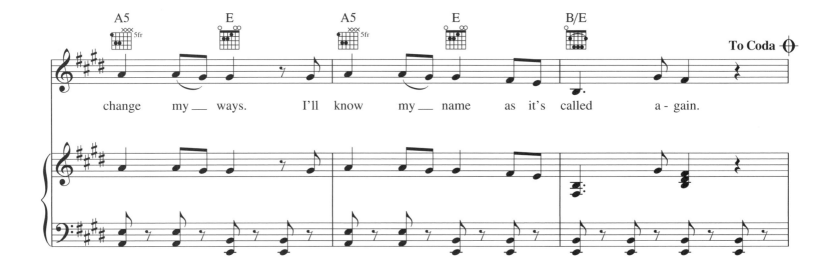

change my __ ways. I'll know my __ name as it's called a - gain.

To Coda ⊕

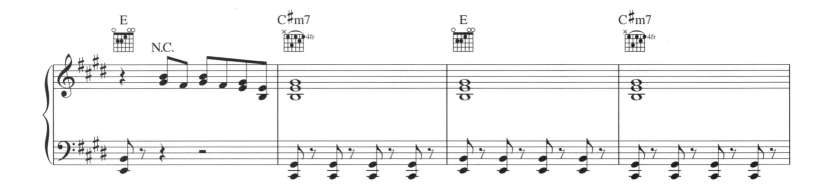

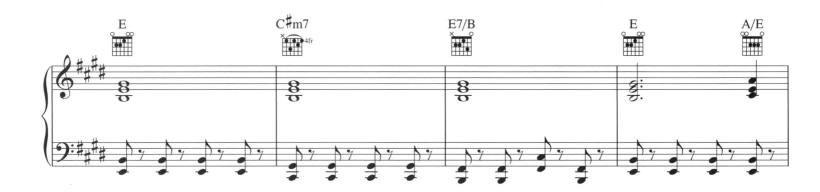

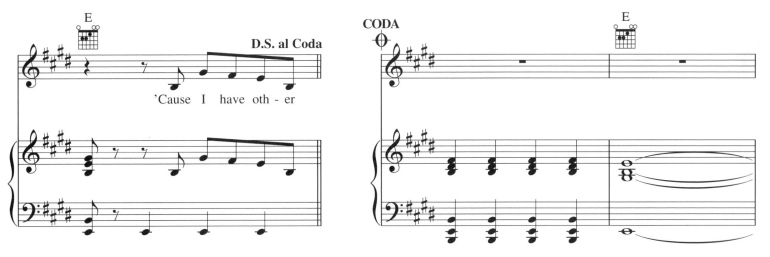

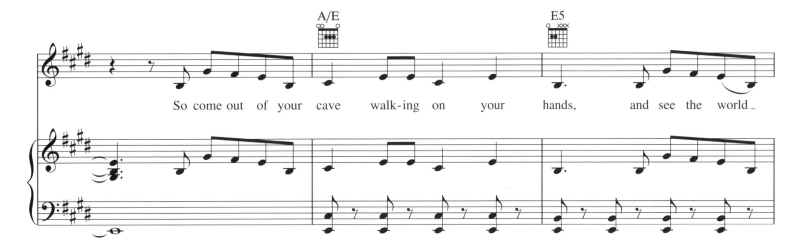

'Cause I have oth-er

So come out of your cave walk-ing on your hands, and see the world

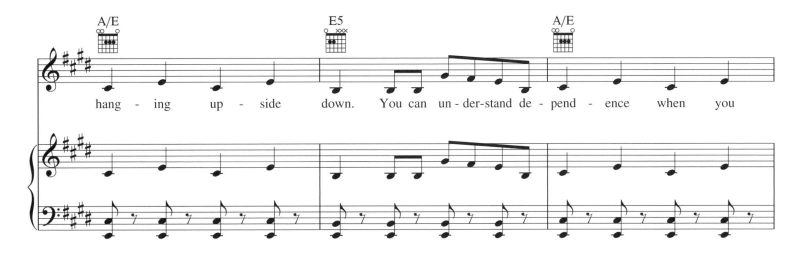

hang-ing up-side down. You can un-der-stand de-pend-ence when you

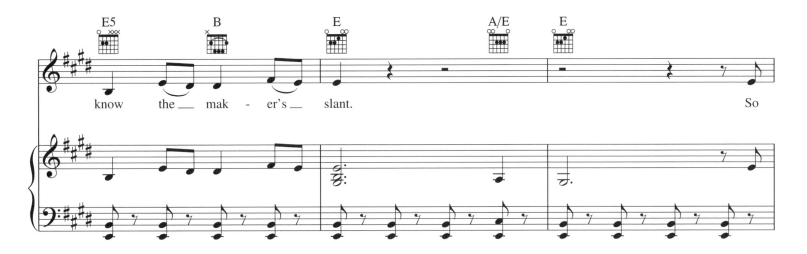

know the __ mak - er's __ slant. So

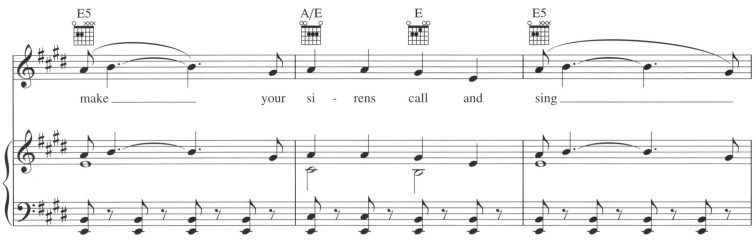

make _____ your si - rens call and sing _____

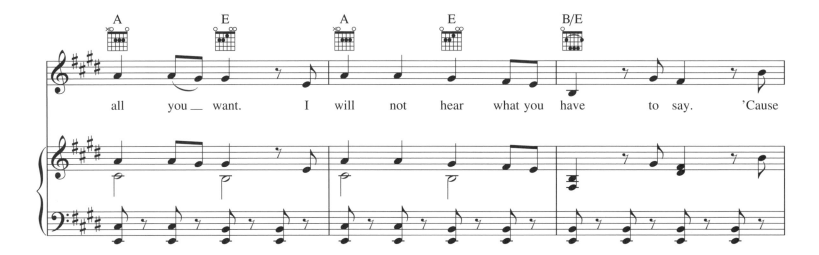

all you __ want. I will not hear what you have to say. 'Cause

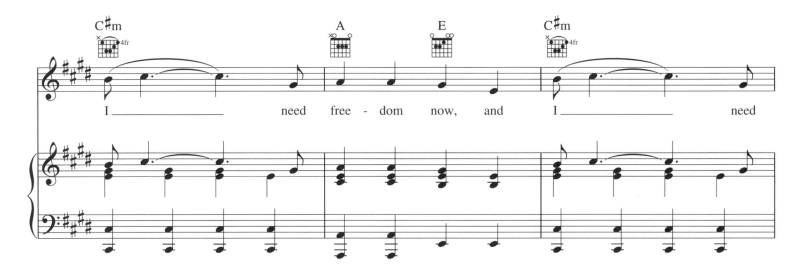

I _____ need free - dom now, and I _____ need

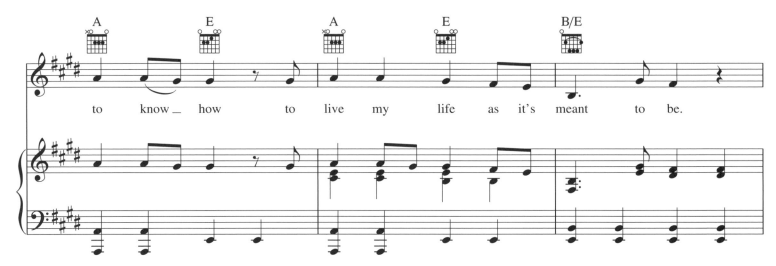

to know __ how to live my life as it's meant to be.

Backing vocals: (Ah, _____ ah, _____

ah. _____ Ah, _____

ah, _____ ah.) _____

And I _____ will hold on hope, and

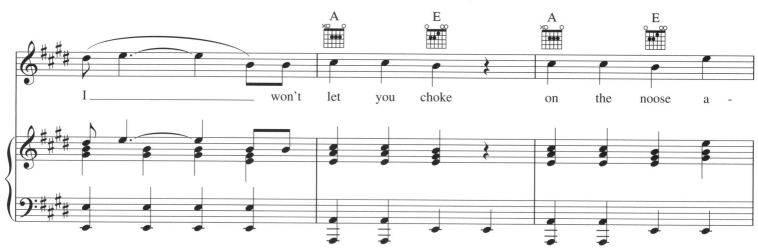

I _____ won't let you choke on the noose a-

round your neck. And I'll _____ find strength in pain, and

I _____ will change my ___ ways. I'll know my ___ name as it's

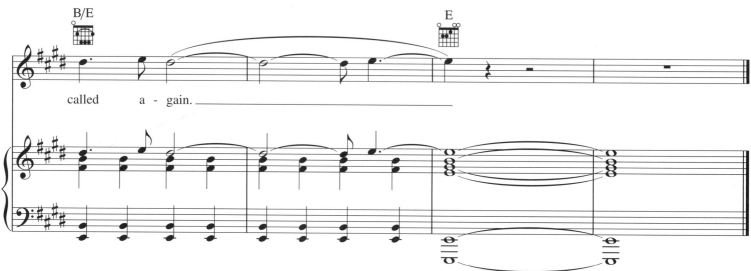

called a - gain. _____

WINTER WINDS

Words and Music by
MUMFORD & SONS

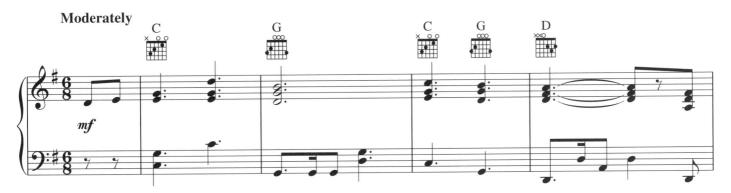

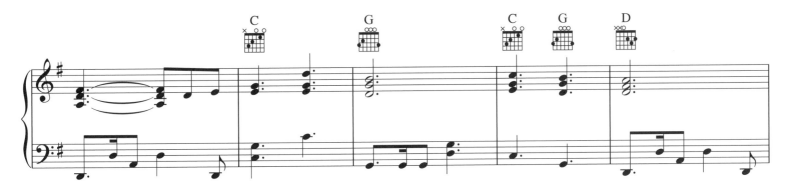

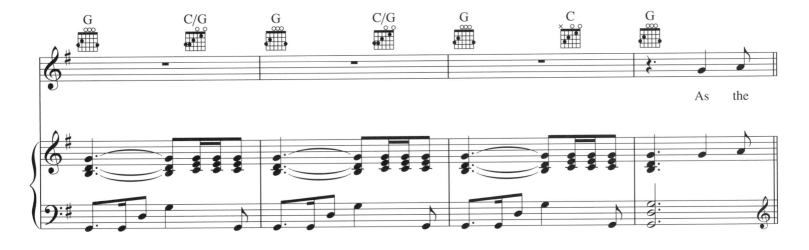

As the

win - ter _____ winds lit - ter Lon-don with lone - ly hearts, ___ oh, the

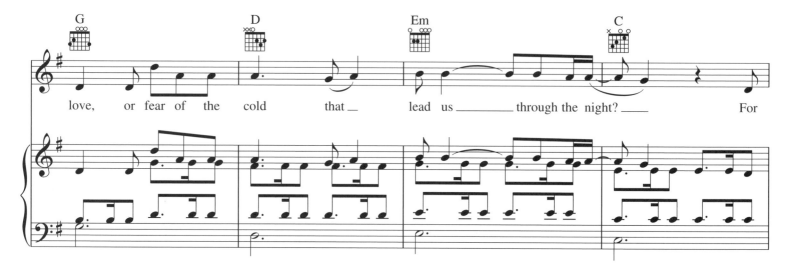

warmth in ___ your eyes swept me in - to ___ your arms. _____ Was it

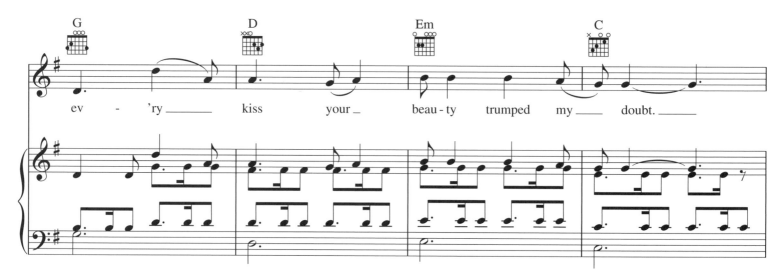

love, or fear of the cold that ___ lead us _____ through the night? _____ For

ev - 'ry _____ kiss your ___ beau-ty trumped my ____ doubt. _____

And my ____ head told my heart: ___ "Let love

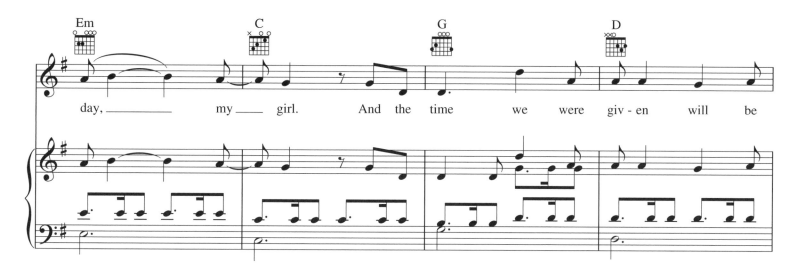

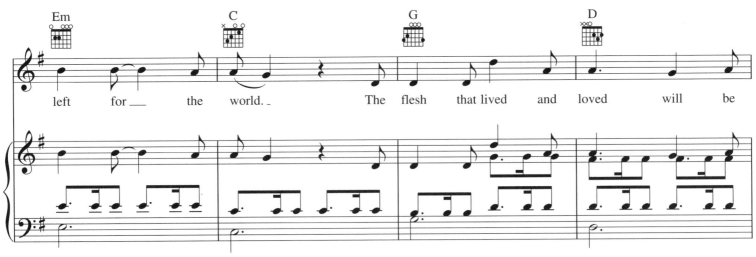

left for ___ the world. ___ The flesh that lived and loved will be

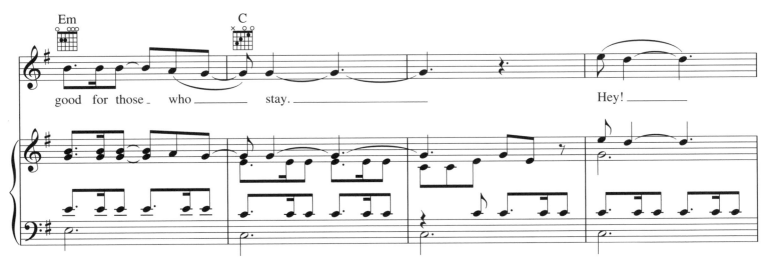

eat - en ___ by plague. ___ So let the mem - o - ries be ___

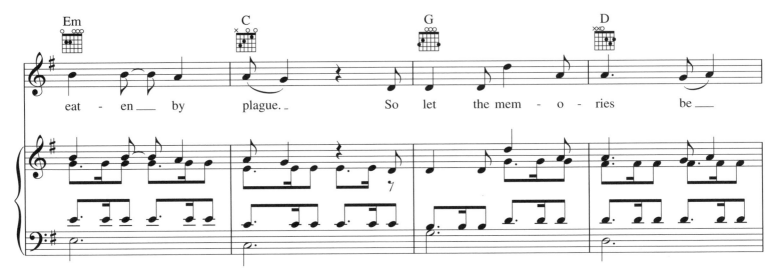

good for those _ who ___ stay. ___ Hey! ___

And my ___ head told my heart: _ "Let love

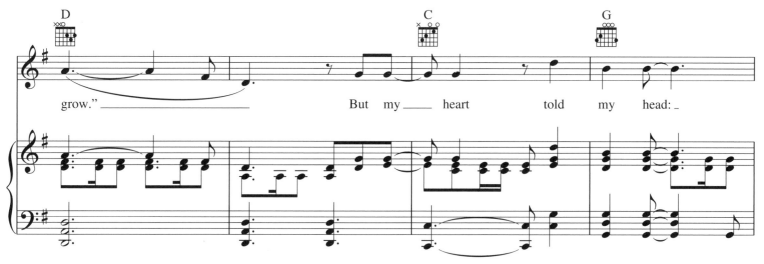

grow." _____ But my ___ heart told my head: _

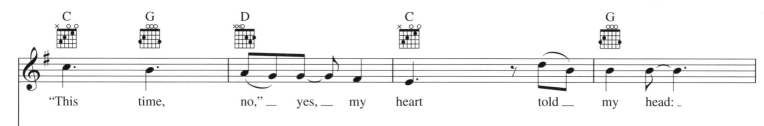

"This time, no," __ yes, __ my heart told __ my head: _

"This time, no, __ this __ time _____ no."

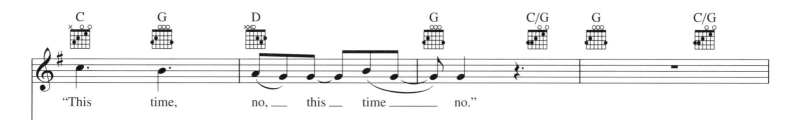

Oh, the shame that sent me off from the

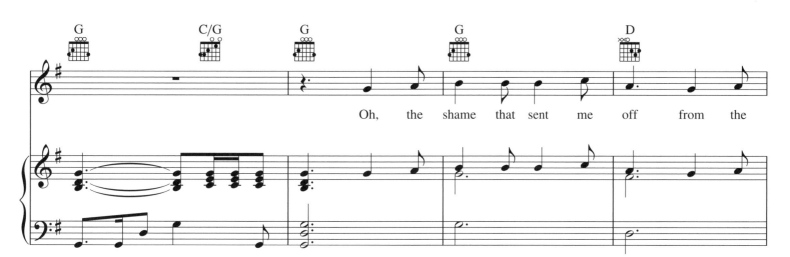

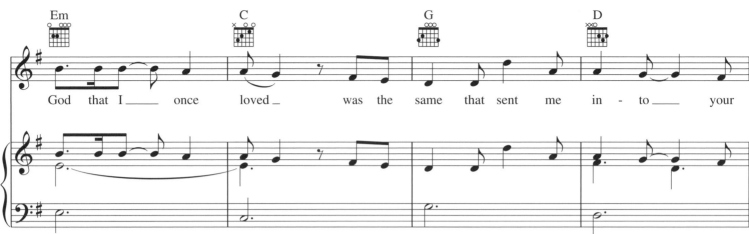

God that I ____ once loved ____ was the same that sent me in - to ____ your

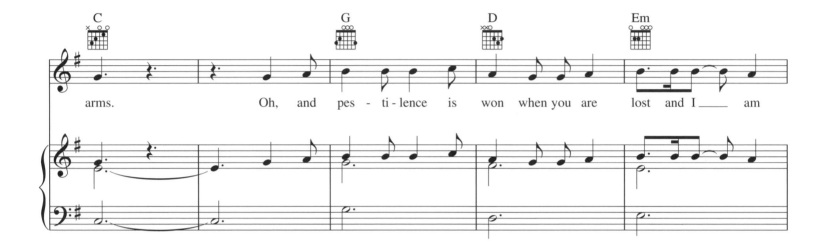

arms. Oh, and pes - ti - lence is won when you are lost and I ____ am

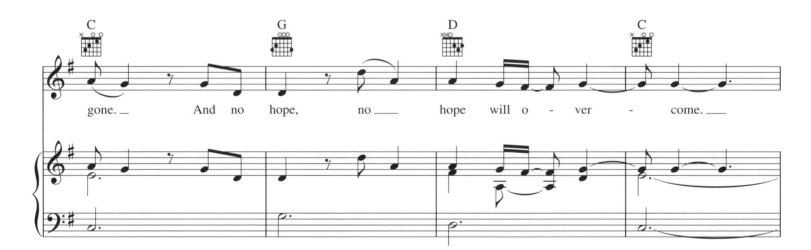

gone. ____ And no hope, no ____ hope will o - ver - come. ____

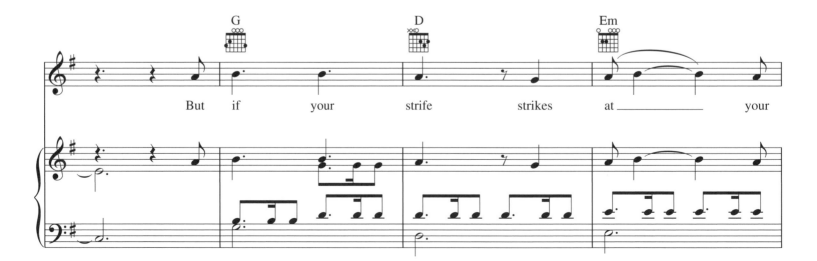

But if your strife strikes at _____ your

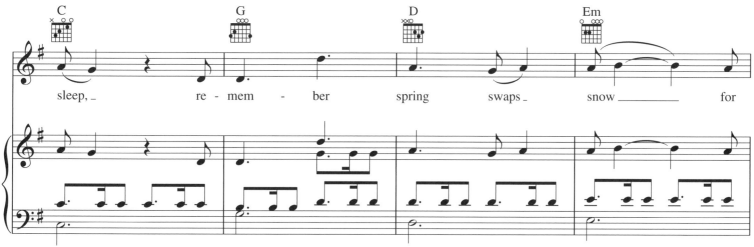

sleep, _ re - mem - ber spring swaps _ snow _____ for

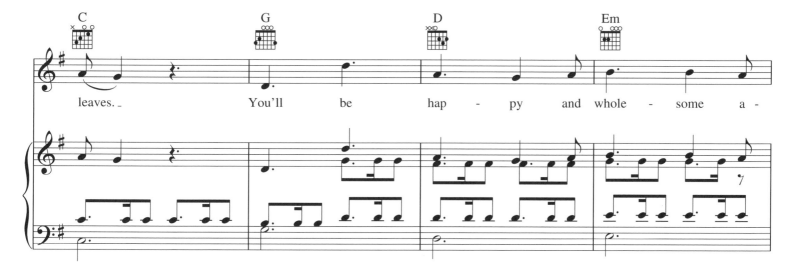

leaves. _ You'll be hap - py and whole - some a -

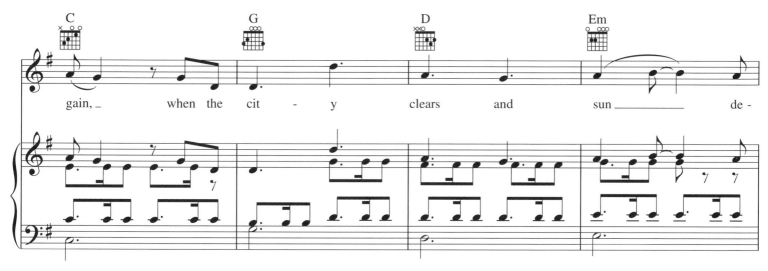

gain, _ when the cit - y clears and sun _____ de -

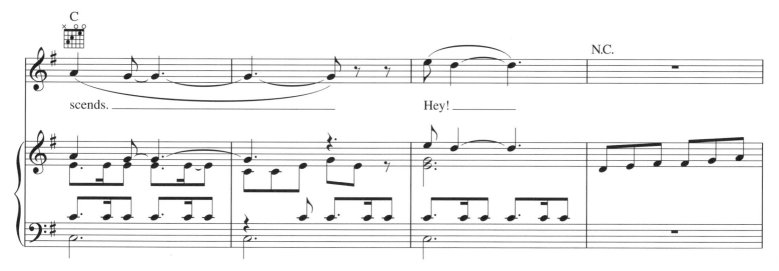

scends. _____ Hey! _____

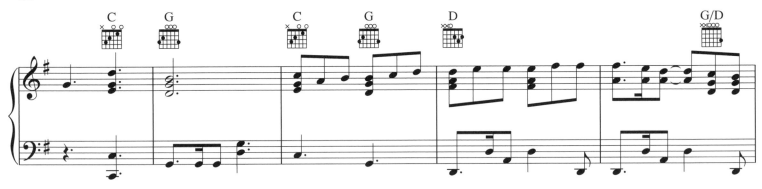

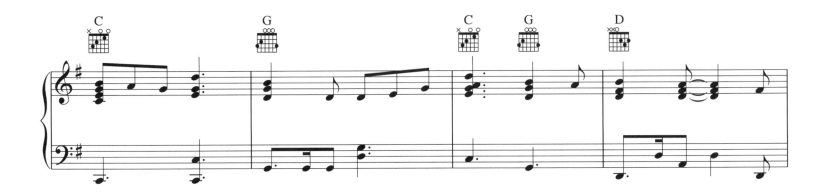

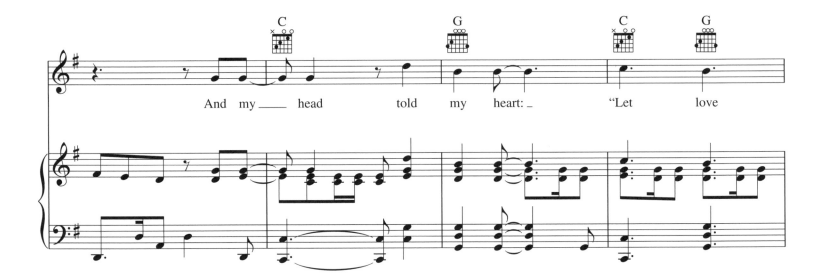

And my ____ head told my heart: _ "Let love

grow." _____ But my ____ heart told my head: _

"This time, no." _____ And my ___ head told

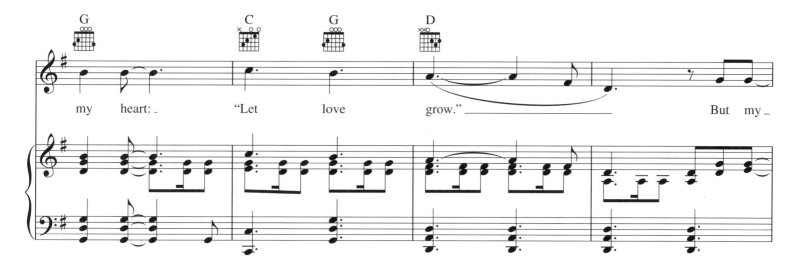

my heart: _ "Let love grow." _____ But my _

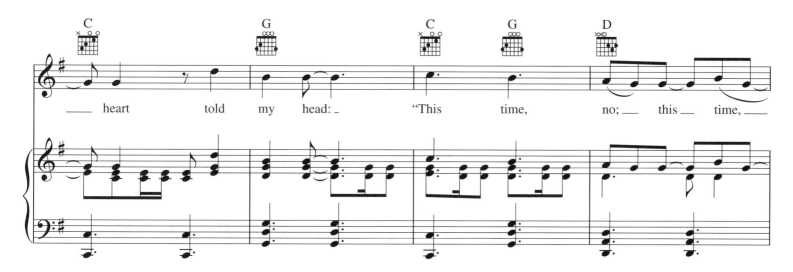

___ heart told my head: _ "This time, no; ___ this ___ time, ___

___ no." _____ Oh. _____

ROLL AWAY YOUR STONE

Words and Music by
MUMFORD & SONS

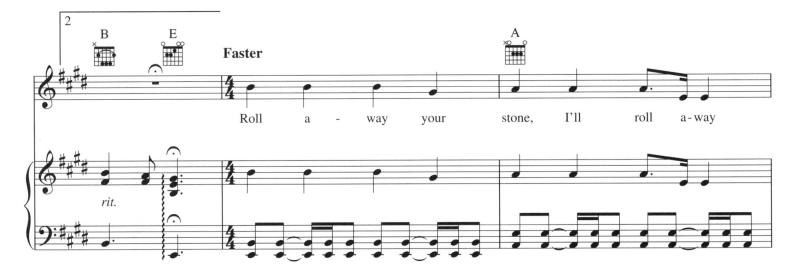

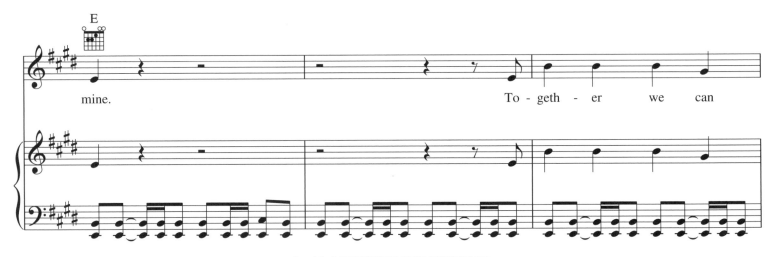

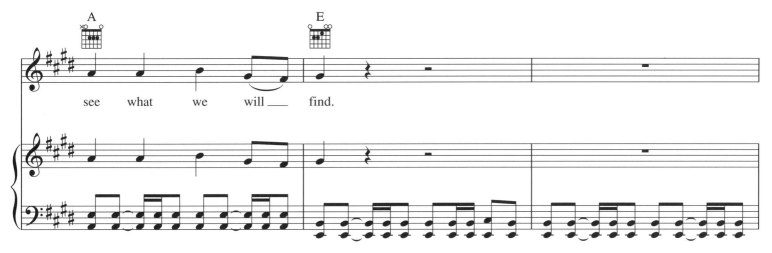

see what we will ___ find.

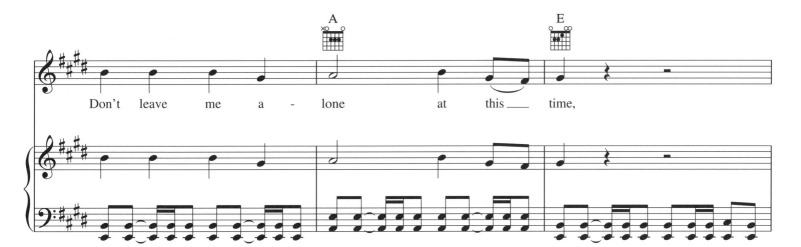

Don't leave me a - lone at this ___ time,

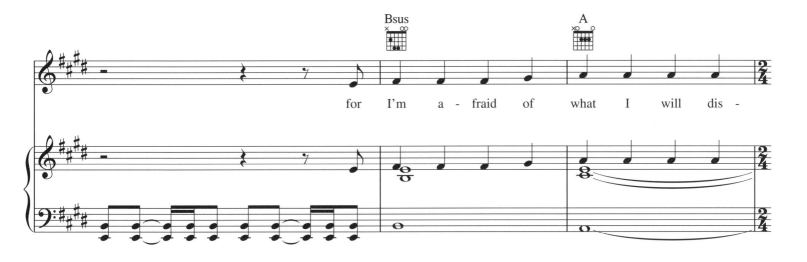

for I'm a - fraid of what I will dis -

cov - er in - side.

'Cause you told me that I would find a _____
seems that all my bridg - es have been _

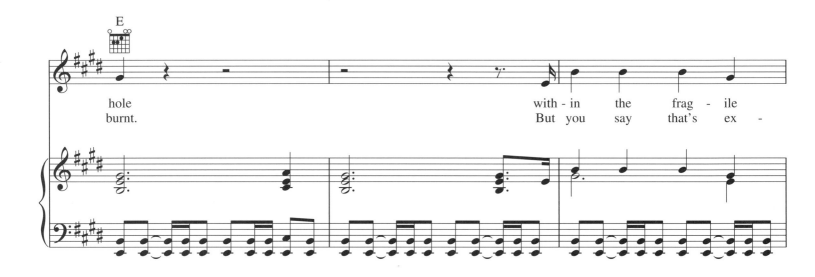

hole
burnt.

with - in the frag - ile
But you say that's ex -

sub - stance of my soul.
act - ly how this grace thing works.

And
It's

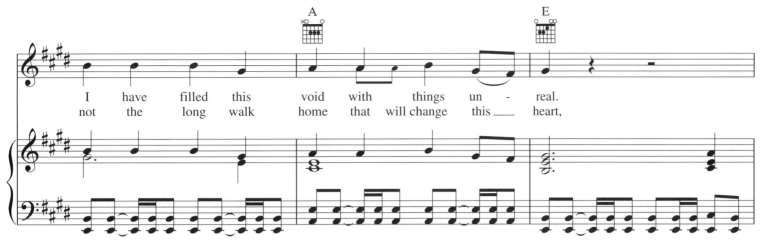

I have filled this void with things un - real.
not the long walk home that will change this ___ heart,

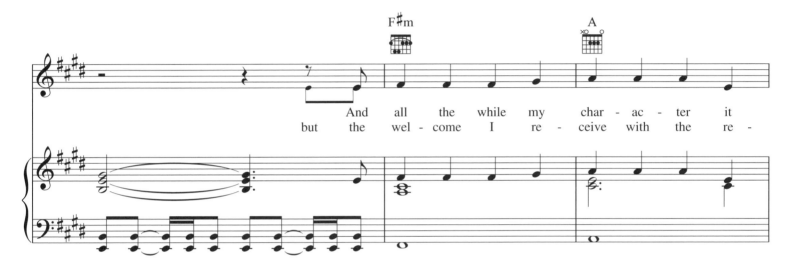

And all the while my char - ac - ter it
but the wel - come I re - ceive with the re -

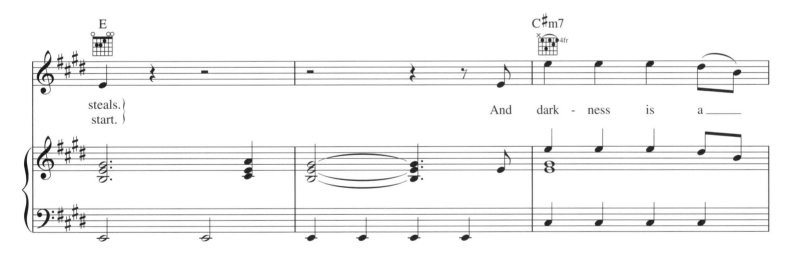

steals.
start.
And dark - ness is a ___

harsh term, don't you think?
And

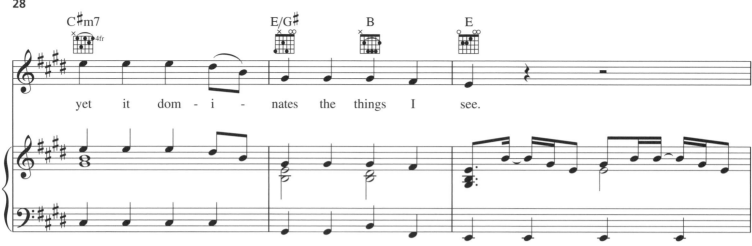

yet it dom - i - nates the things I see.

1

It

2

And dark - ness is a ____ harsh term, don't you

think?

And yet it dom - i -

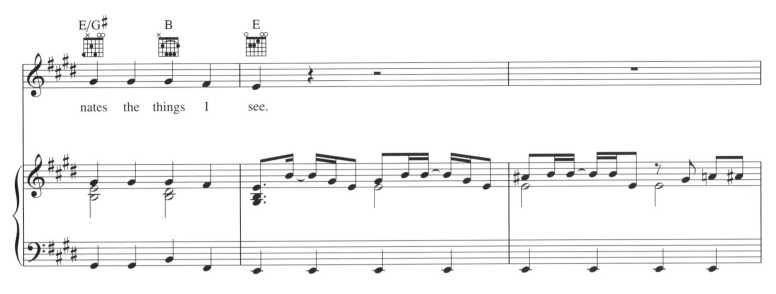

nates the things I see.

Tempo I

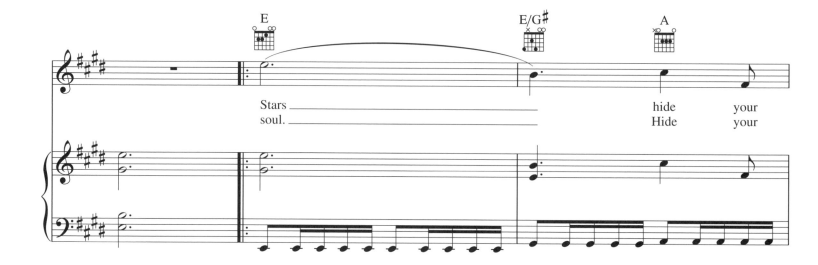

Stars _____ hide your
soul. _____ Hide your

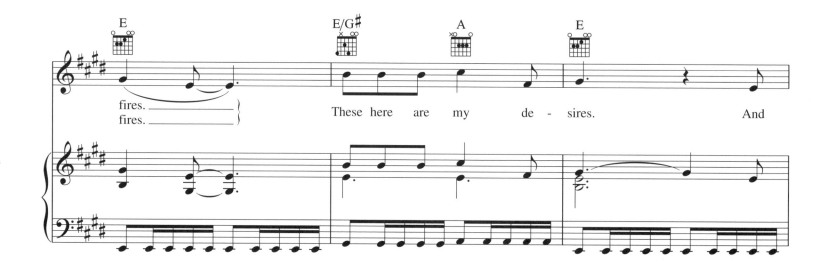

fires. _____ These here are my de - sires. And
fires. _____

I will give them up to you this time a - round. And

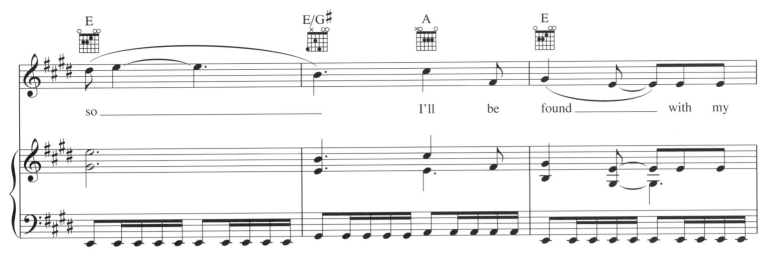

so _____ I'll be found _____ with my

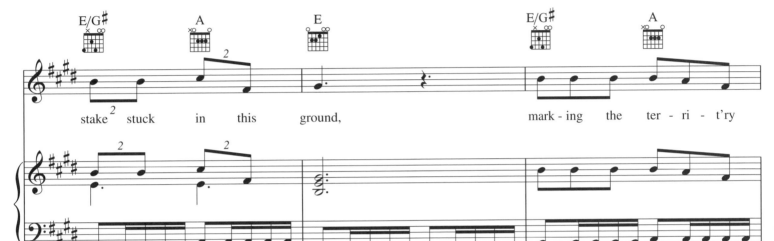

stake stuck in this ground, mark - ing the ter - ri - t'ry

of ___ this new - ly im - pas - sioned soul. _____

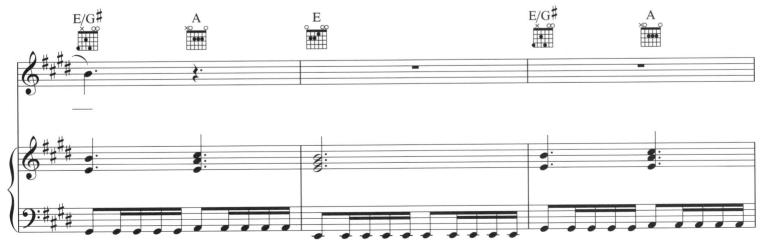

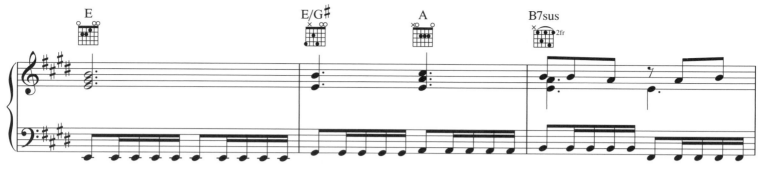

But you, you've

gone too far this time. You have nei - ther rea - son nor rhyme with

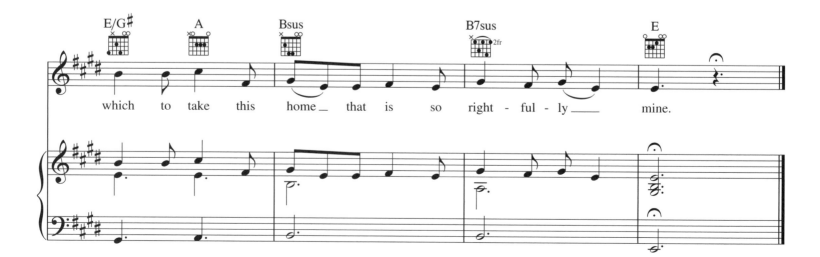

which to take this home __ that is so right - ful - ly ____ mine.

WHITE BLANK PAGE

Words and Music by
MUMFORD & SONS

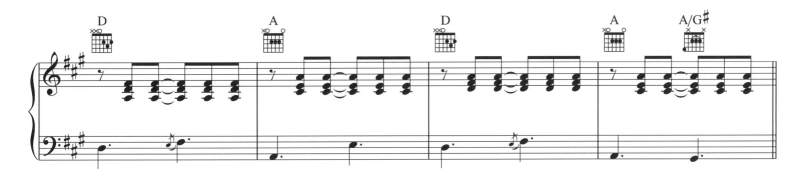

Can you lie next to her and give her your
A white blank page and a swell-ing

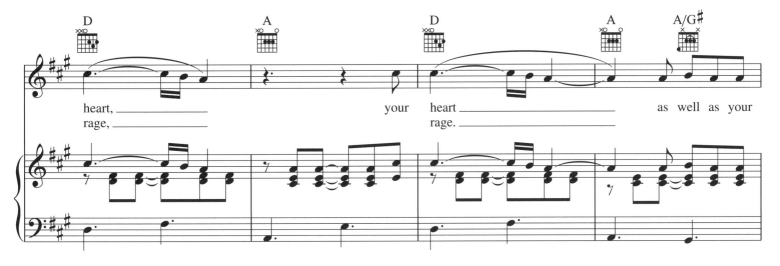

heart, _____ your heart _____ as well as your
rage, _____ rage. _____

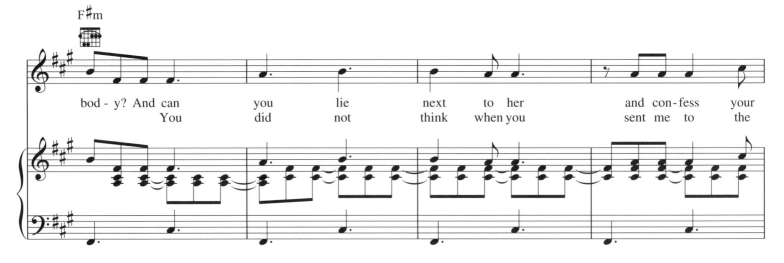

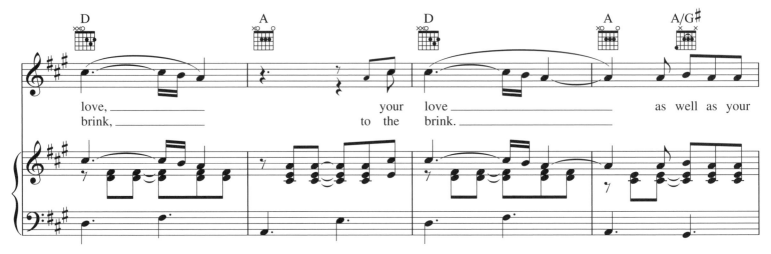

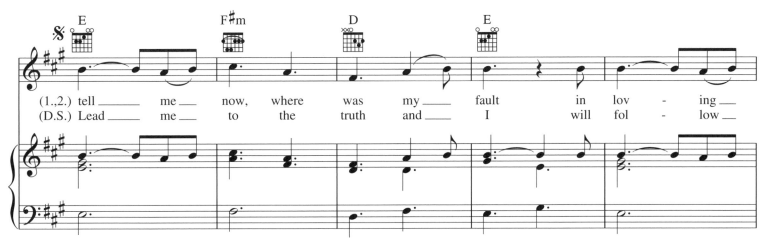

(1.,2.) tell ____ me ____ now, where was my ____ fault in lov - ing ____
(D.S.) Lead ____ me ____ to the was truth and ____ I will fol - low ____

you with my whole ____ heart? Oh, tell ____ me ____ now, where
you with my whole ____ life. Oh, lead ____ me ____ to the

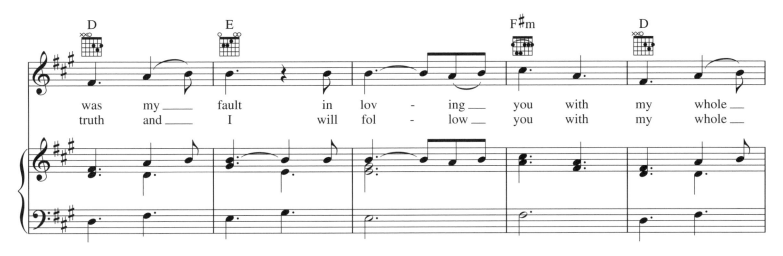

was my ____ fault in lov - ing ____ you with my whole ____
truth and ____ I will fol - low ____ you with my whole ____

To Coda ⊕

heart?
life.

8vb

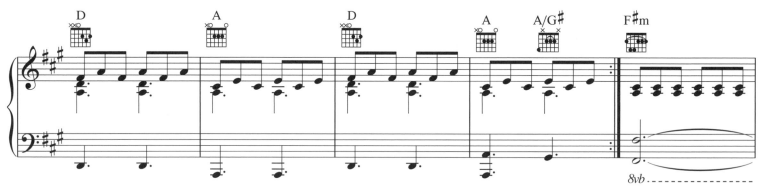

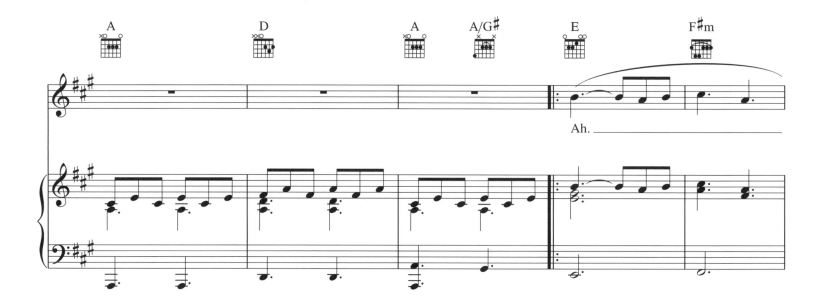

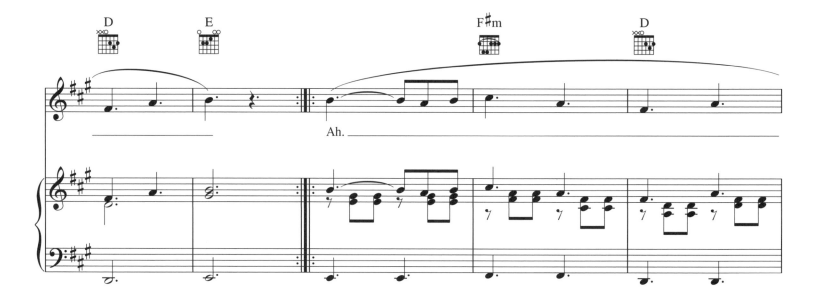

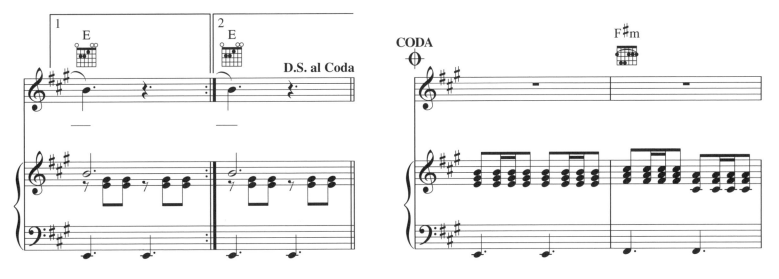

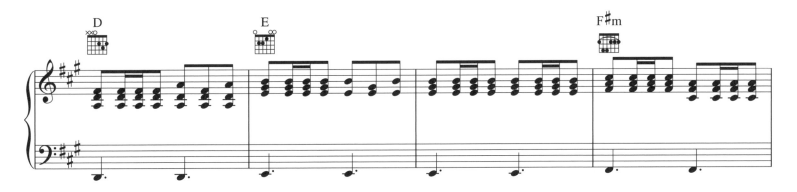

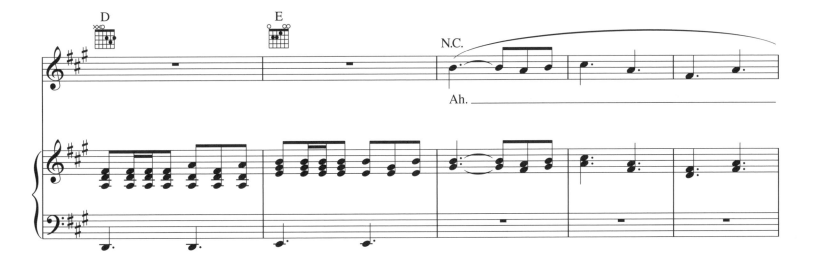

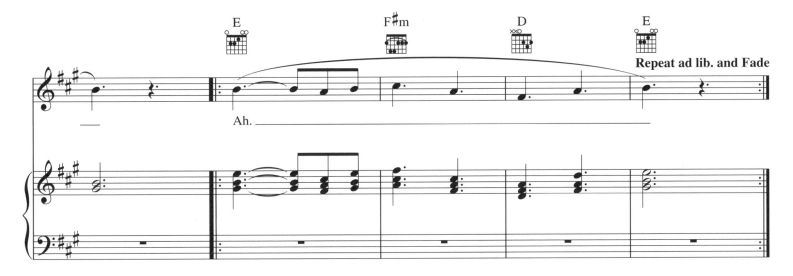

I GAVE YOU ALL

Words and Music by
MUMFORD & SONS

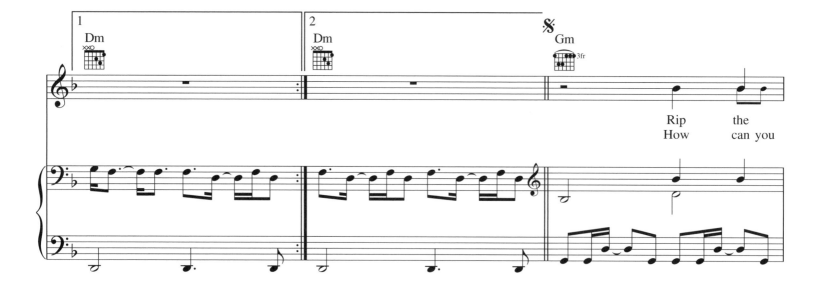

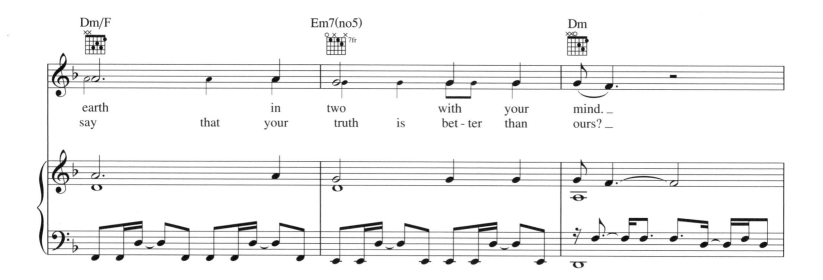

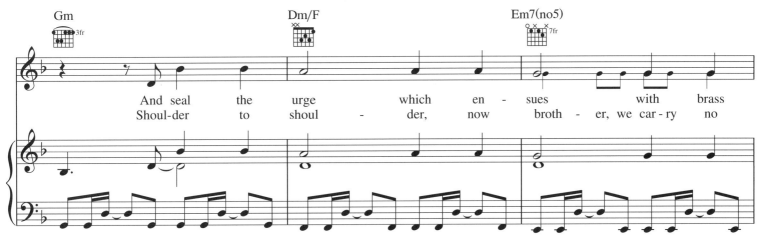

Gm   Dm/F   Em7(no5)

And seal the urge which en - sues with brass
Shoul-der to shoul - der, now broth - er, we car - ry no

Dm   Gm   Dm/F C

wires. _ I nev - er meant you an - y _
arms. _ The blind man sleeps in the door-way, his _

Dm   Gm   Dm/F

harm. Your tears feel warm as they
home. If on - ly I had an en-e-my big-ger than my

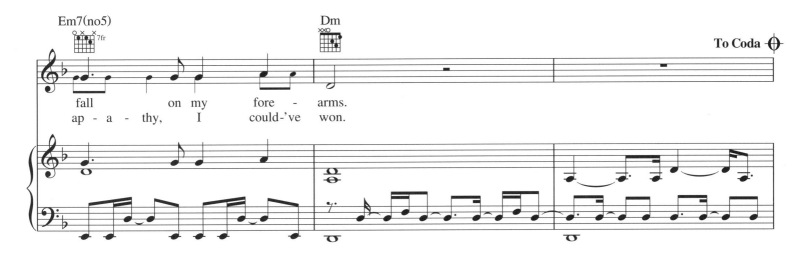

Em7(no5)   Dm   **To Coda** ⊕

fall on my fore - arms.
ap - a - thy, I could-'ve won.

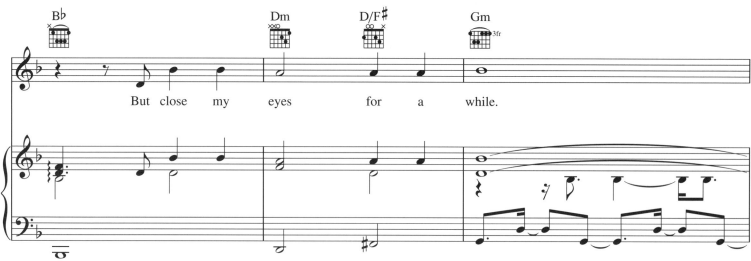

But close my eyes for a while.

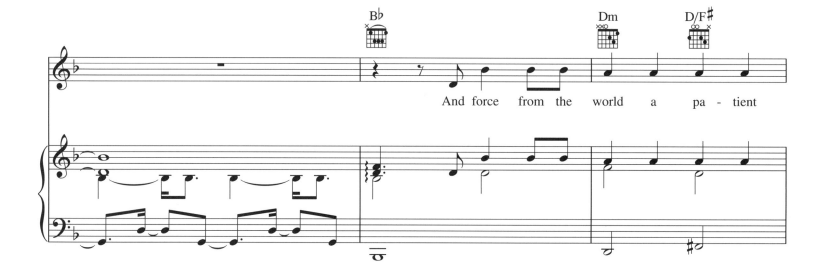

And force from the world a pa - tient

smile.

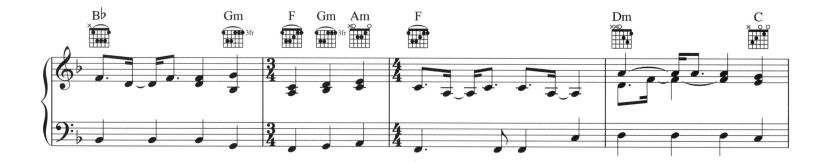

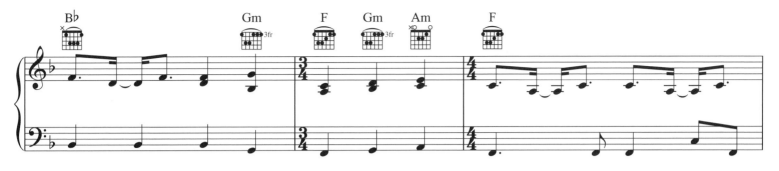

D.S. al Coda

CODA

But I gave you all.

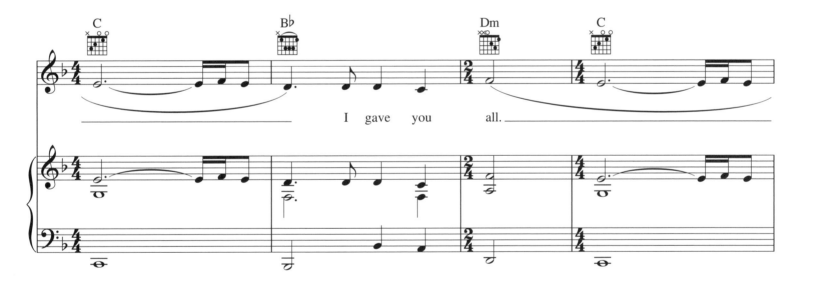

I gave you all.

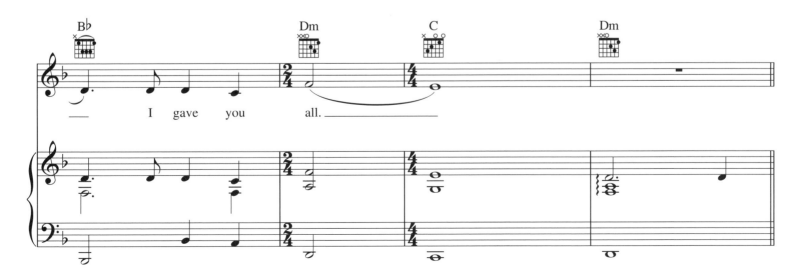

I gave you all.

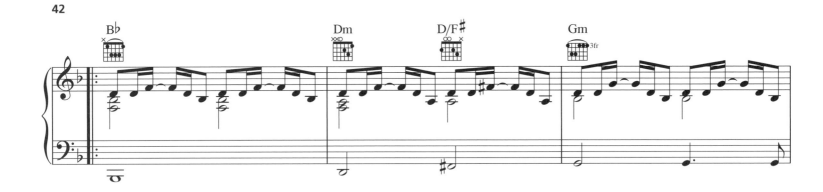

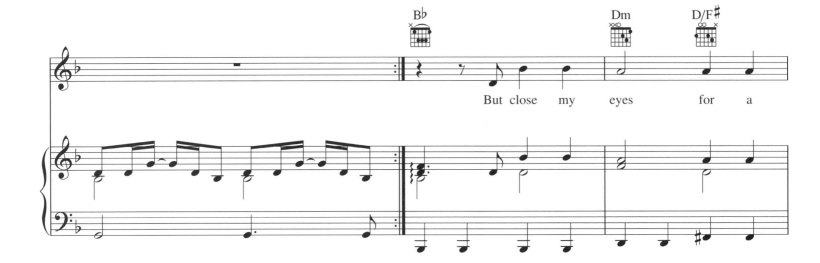

But close my eyes for a

while. And force from the

world a pa - tient smile.

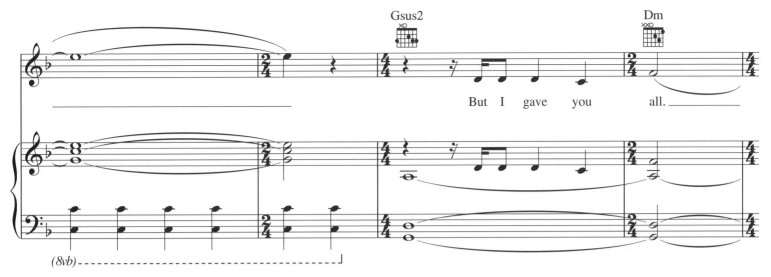

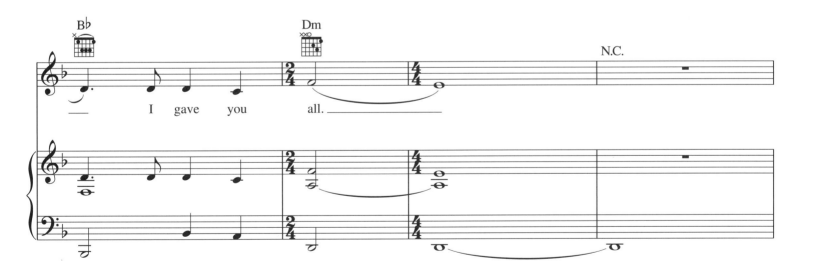

LITTLE LION MAN

Words and Music by
MUMFORD & SONS

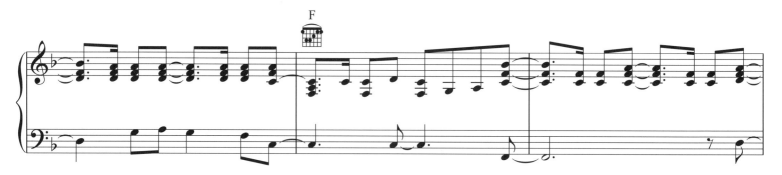

Weep for your-self, my man, you'll nev - er be what is in your _

_ heart. _____ Weep, lit - tle li - on man, you're

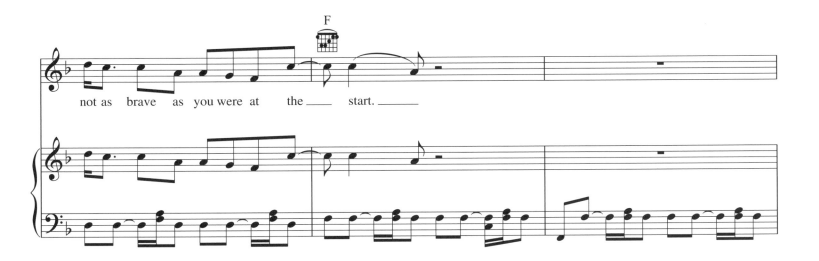

not as brave as you were at the ____ start. _____

Rate your-self and rape your-self, take all the cour-age you have ___ left.

And waste it on fix-ing all the prob-lems that you made in your own ___

___ head. But it was not your fault, but mine. ___

And it was your heart on the line. ___ I real - ly

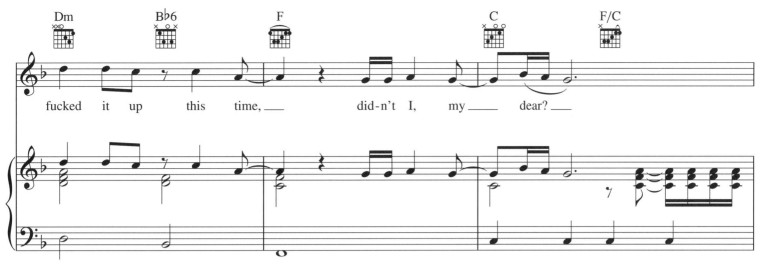

fucked it up this time, ___ did-n't I, my ___ dear? ___

Did-n't I, my...

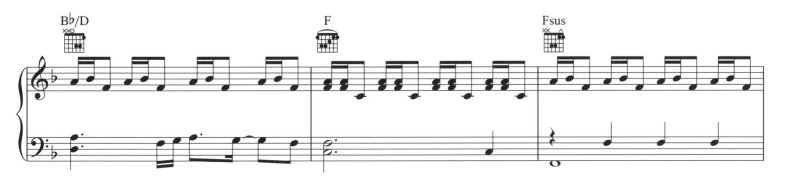

Trem-ble for your-self, my man, you know that you have seen this all be - fore._____

Trem-ble lit-tle li - on man. You'll nev-er set - tle an-y of your_

_____ scores. _____ Your grace is wast - ed in your face, your

bold-ness stands a-lone a-mong the wreck. Now

learn from your moth-er or else spend your days bit - ing __ your own __ neck.

But it was not your fault, but mine. __ And it was

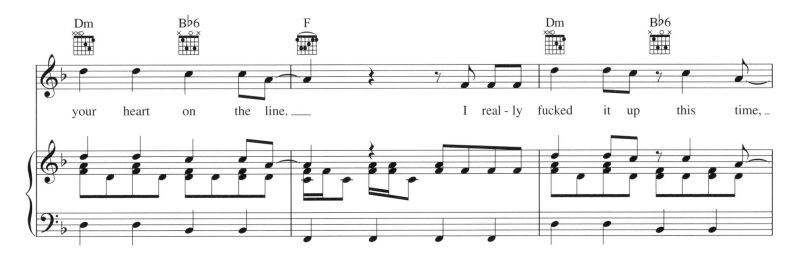

your heart on the line. __ I real - ly fucked it up this time, __

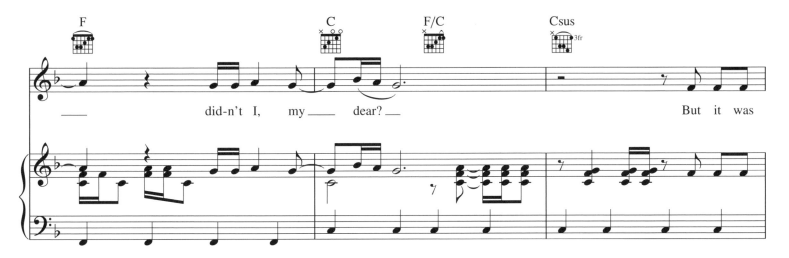

__ did-n't I, my __ dear? __ But it was

not your fault, but mine. ___ And it was your heart on the line. _

___ I real-ly fucked it up this time, ___ did-n't I, my _

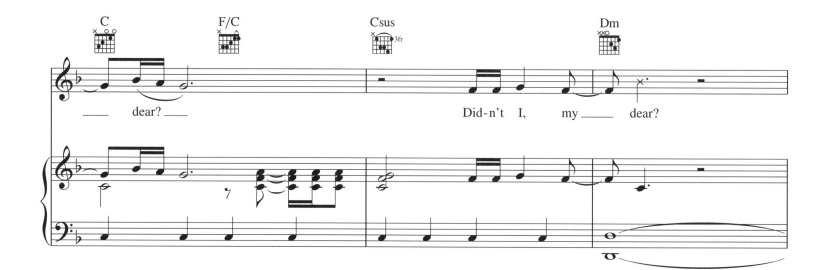

___ dear? ___ Did-n't I, my ___ dear?

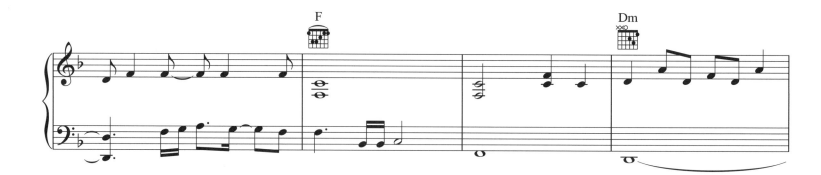

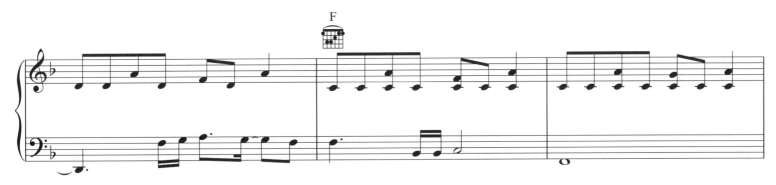

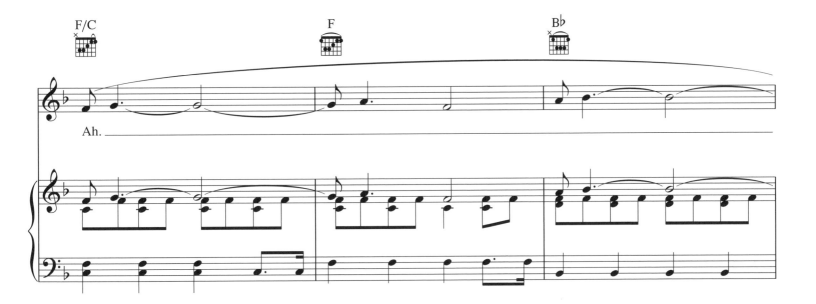

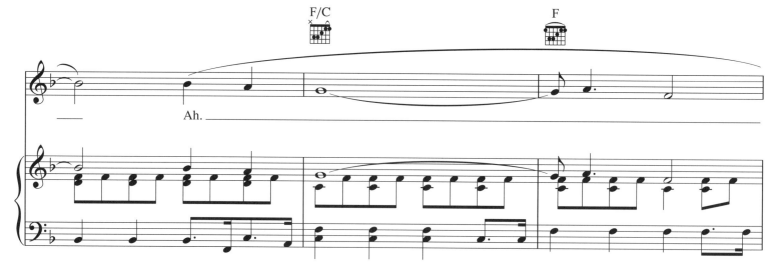

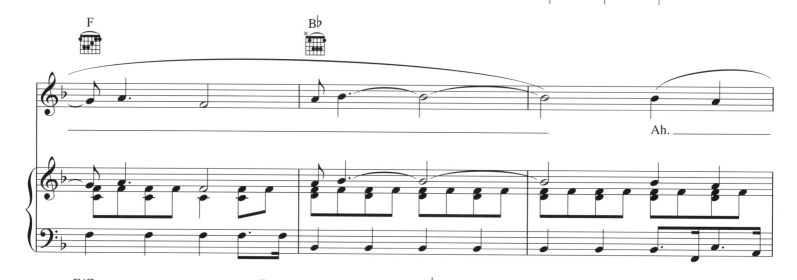

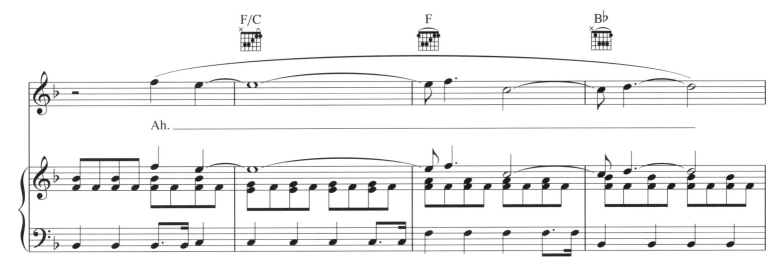

Ah.

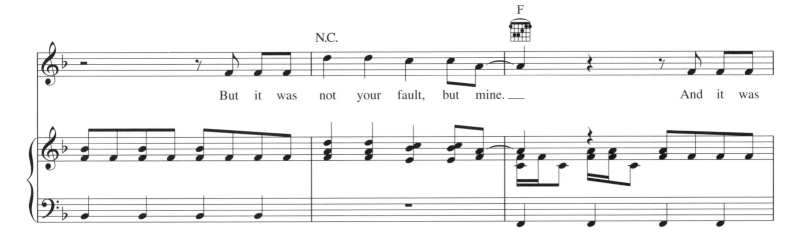

But it was not your fault, but mine. ___ And it was

your heart on the line. ___ I real - ly fucked it up this time, _

did-n't I, my _____ dear? _____ But it was

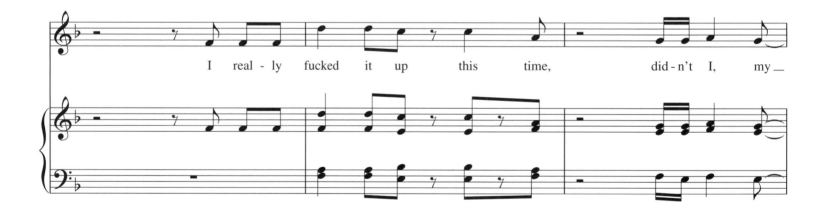

not your fault, but mine. And it was your heart on the line.

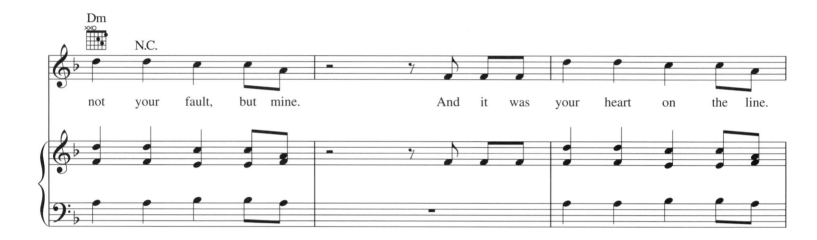

I real-ly fucked it up this time, did-n't I, my _

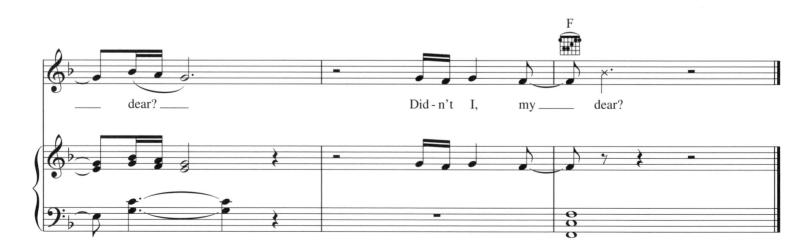

_____ dear? _____ Did-n't I, my _____ dear?

TIMSHEL

Words and Music by
MUMFORD & SONS

Cold is the wa - ter, _____ it
you are the moth - er, _____ the

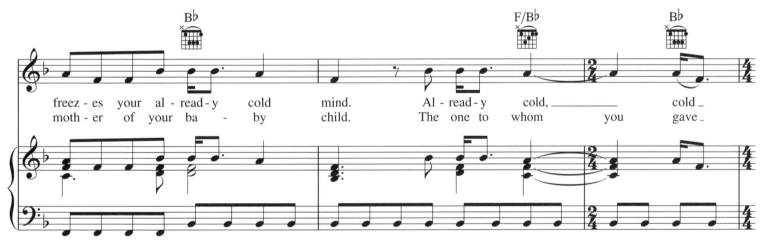

freez - es your al - read - y cold mind. Al - read - y cold, _____ cold ___
moth - er of your ba - by child. The one to whom you gave ___

mind.
life.

Death is at your door - step ___
You have your ___ choic - es ___

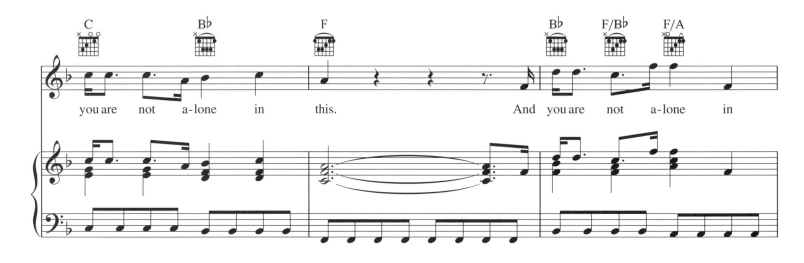

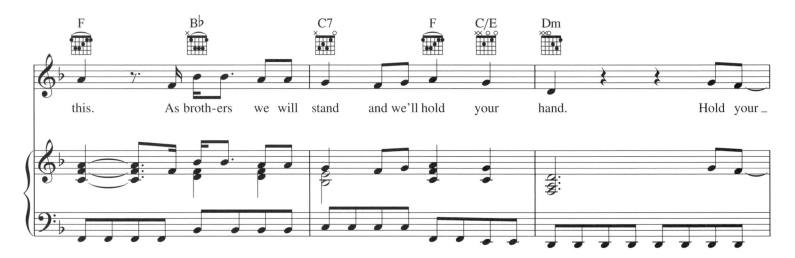

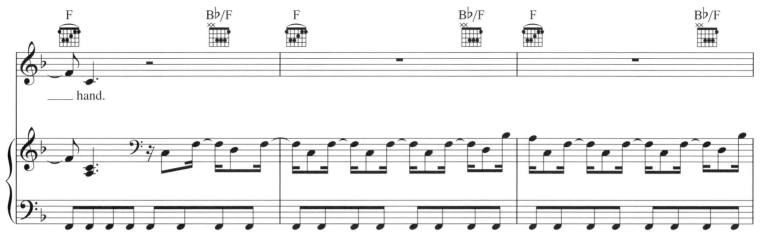

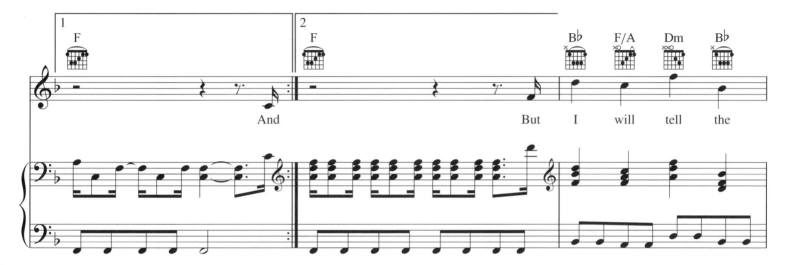

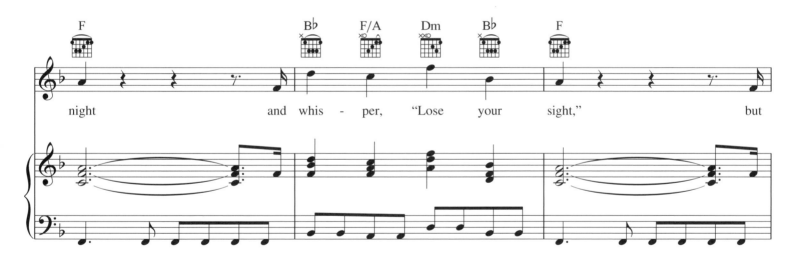

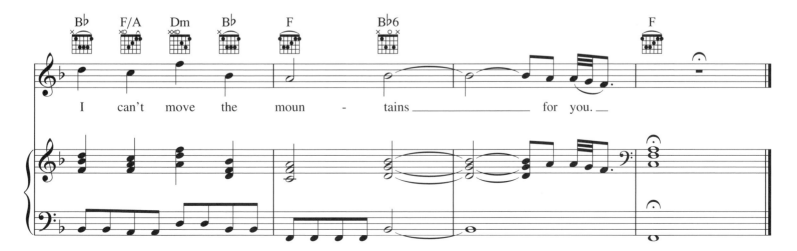

THISTLE AND WEEDS

Words and Music by
MUMFORD & SONS

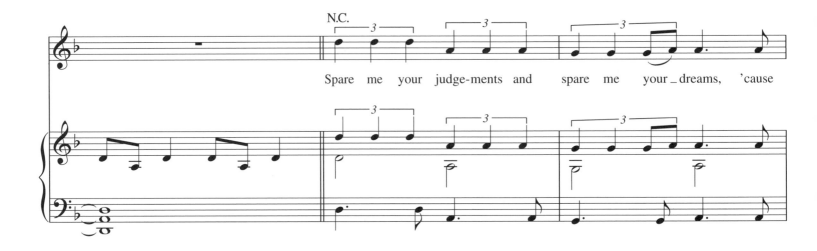

Spare me your judge-ments and spare me your _ dreams, 'cause

re - cent-ly mine have been tear-ing my _ seams. I sit a - lone in this win-ter

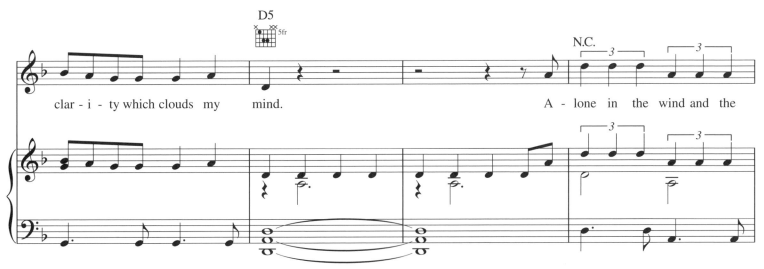

clar - i - ty which clouds my mind. A - lone in the wind and the

rain you left __ me. It's get - ting dark, dar - ling, __ too dark to see. And I'm

on my knees, and your faith in shreds, it seems. __

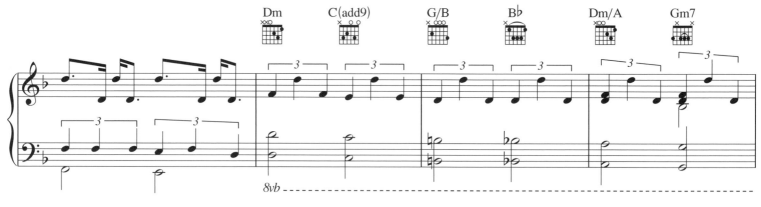

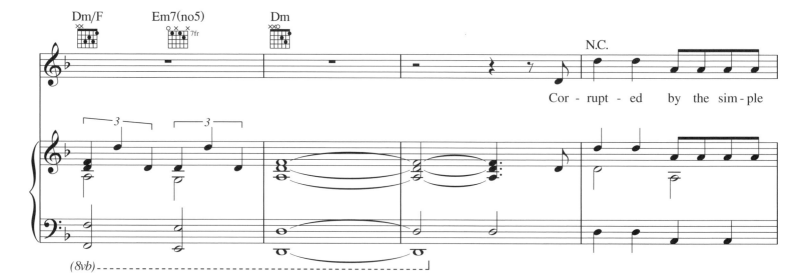

Cor - rupt - ed by the sim - ple

sniff of rich - es blown. I know you have felt much more love that you've _ shown. And I'm

on my knees and the wa - ter creeps to my chest.

Plant your hope with good _____ seeds.   Don't cov-er your-self with
o-ver your hills and   be _____ still.   The sky ____ a-bove us

this-tle and weeds. }   Rain down,   rain down on   me. ____
shoots to kill. }

Look

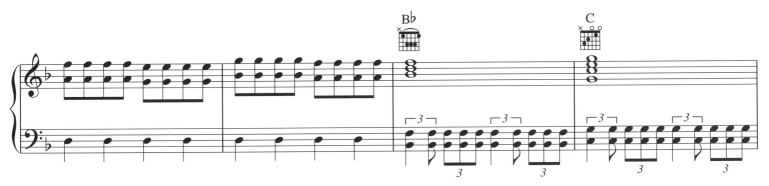

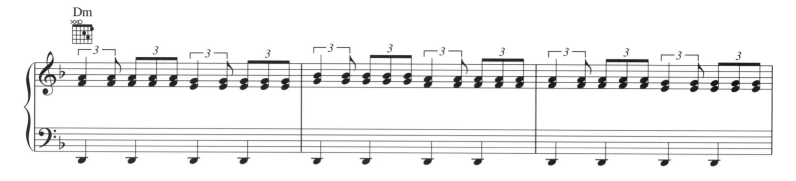

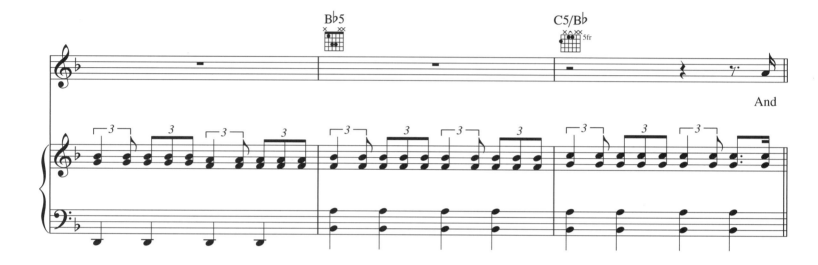

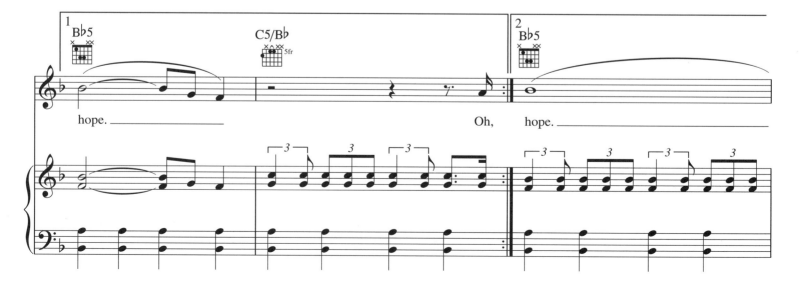

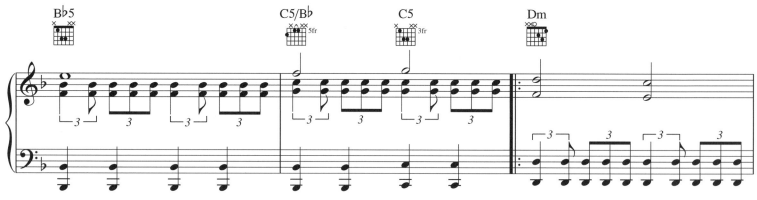

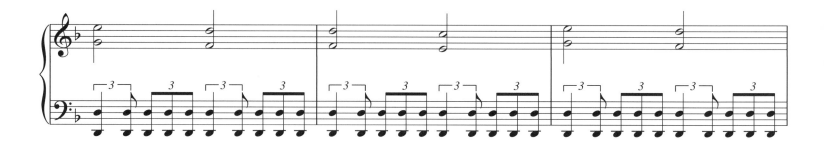

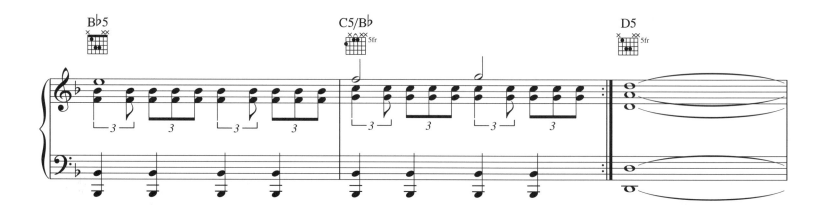

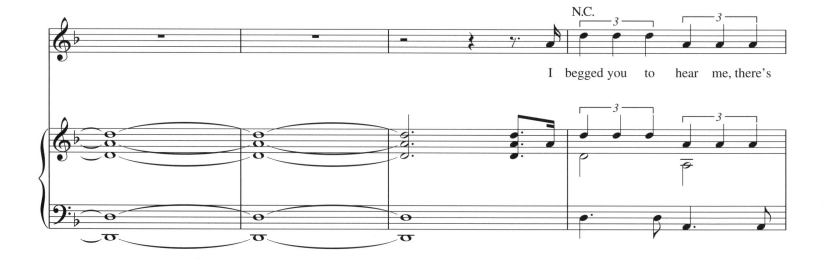

I begged you to hear me, there's

more than flesh and bones. Let the dead bur-y the dead, and they will come out in __ droves. Take the

spade from my hands __ and fill in the holes you've made.

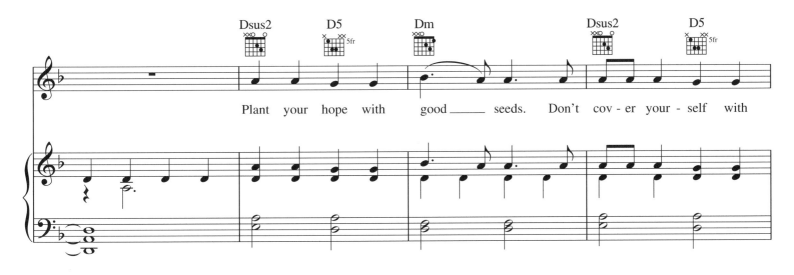

Plant your hope with good _____ seeds. Don't cov-er your-self with

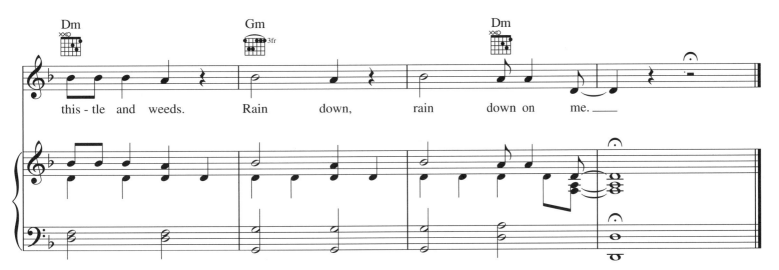

this-tle and weeds. Rain down, rain down on me. ____

AWAKE MY SOUL

Words and Music by
MUMFORD & SONS

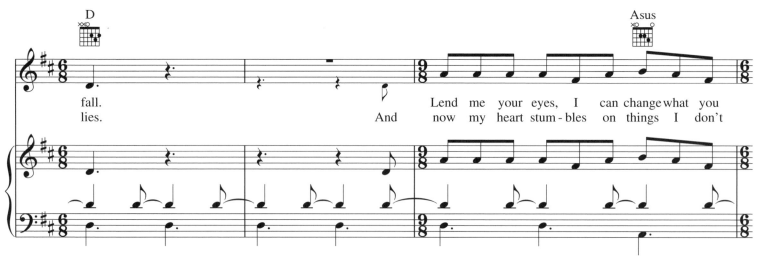

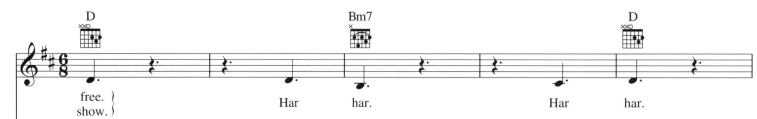

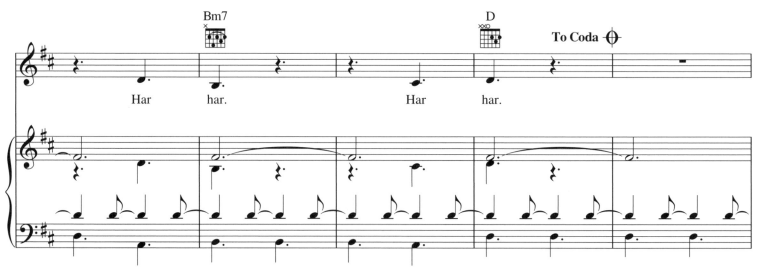

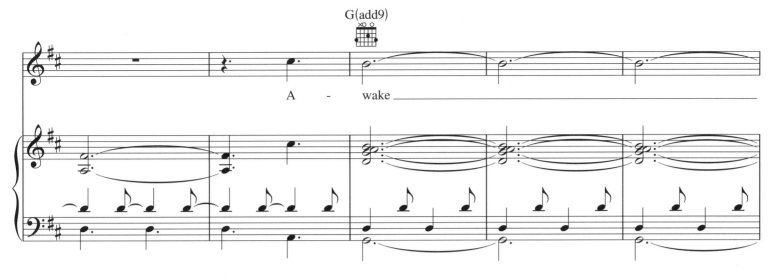

G(add9)

A - wake

D

my soul. A -

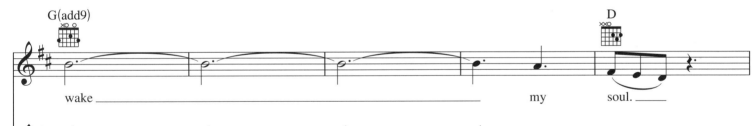

G(add9)   D

wake   my   soul.

D.S. al Coda   **CODA**

How   In these

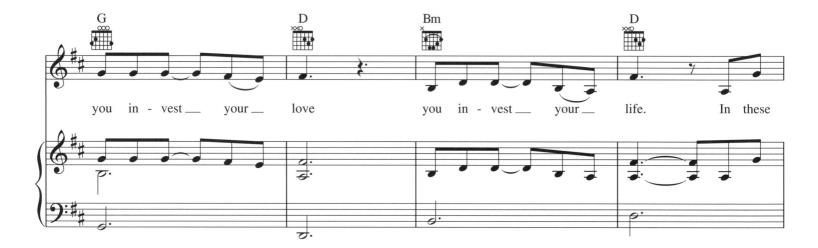

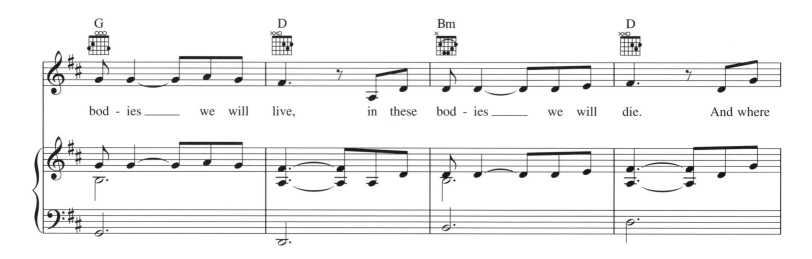

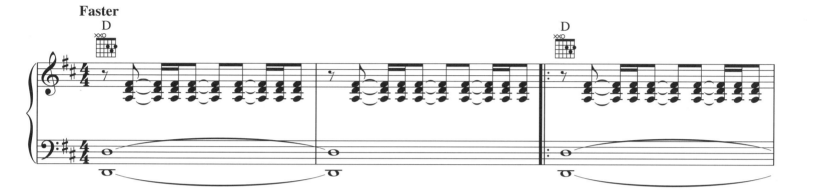

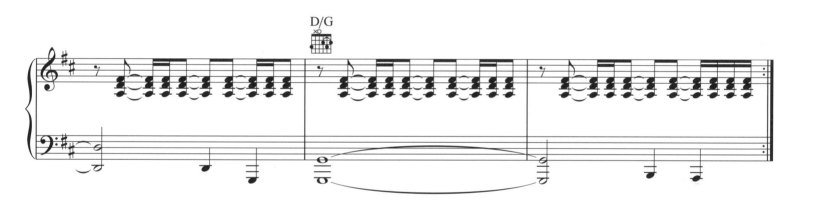

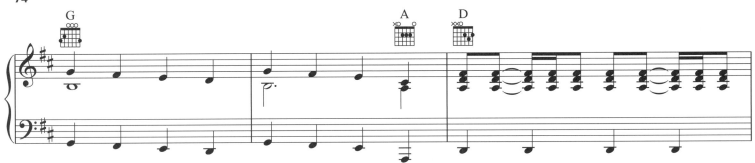

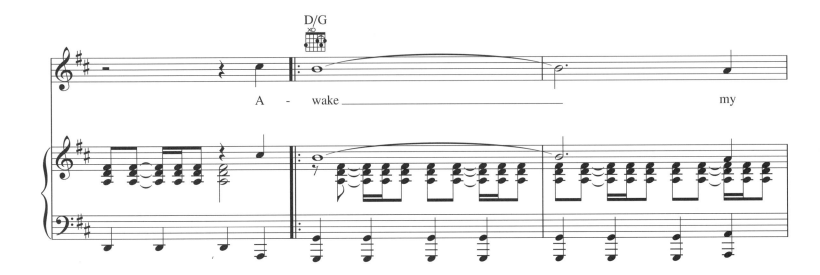

A - wake _____ my

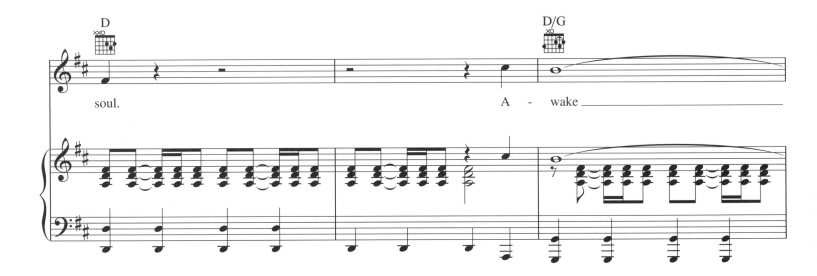

soul.   A - wake _____

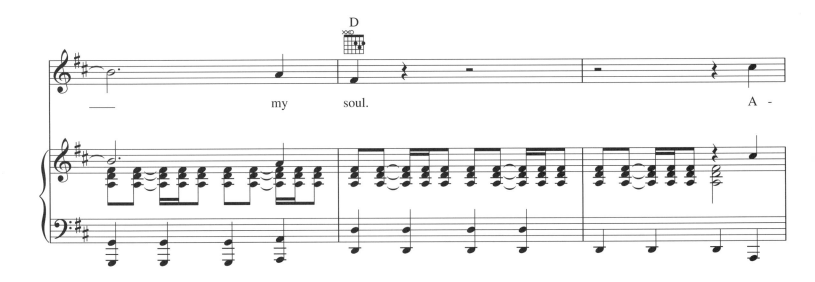

_____ my soul.   A -

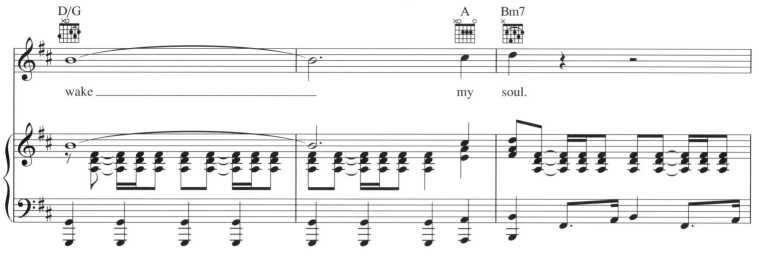

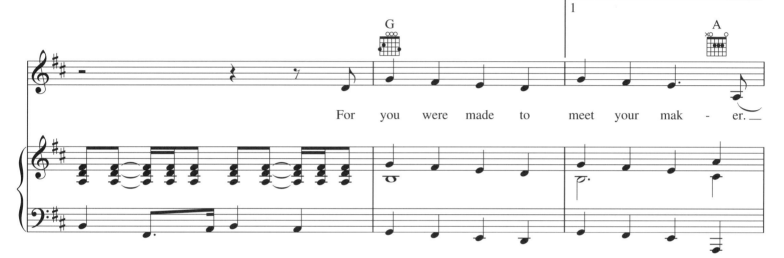

DUST BOWL DANCE

Words and Music by
MUMFORD & SONS

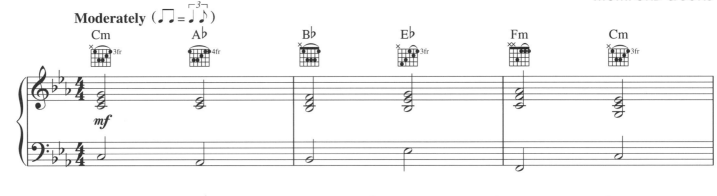

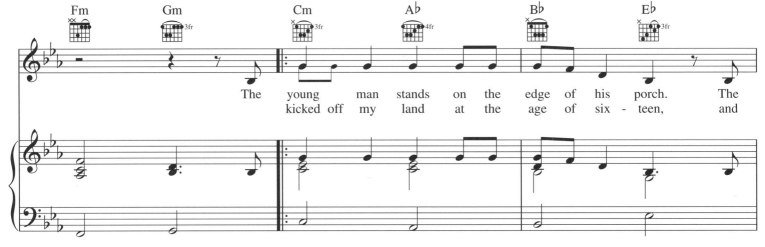

The young man stands on the edge of his porch. The
kicked off my land at the edge of age of six-teen, and

days were _ short and the fa-ther was gone. _ There was no one in the town and
I have no i-dea where else my heart could-'ve been. I placed all my trust at the

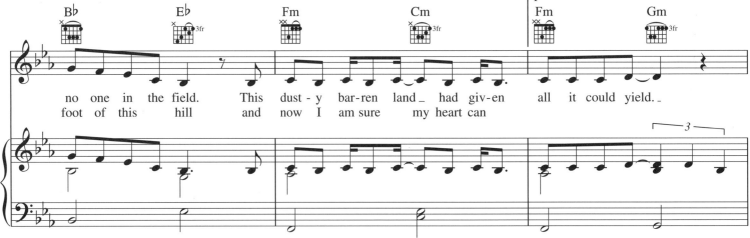

no one in the field. This dust-y bar-ren land _ had giv-en all it could yield. _
foot of this hill and now I am sure my heart can

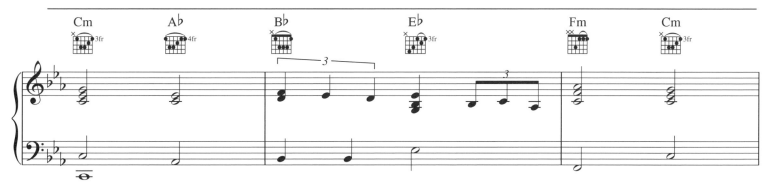

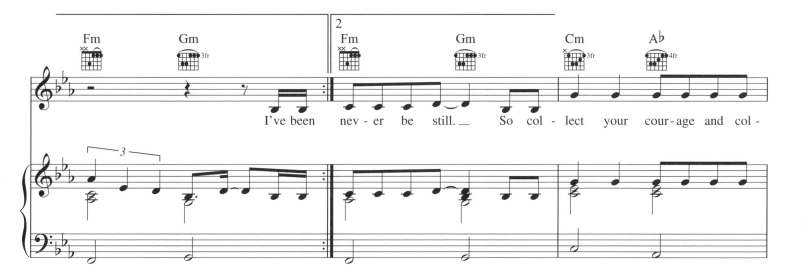

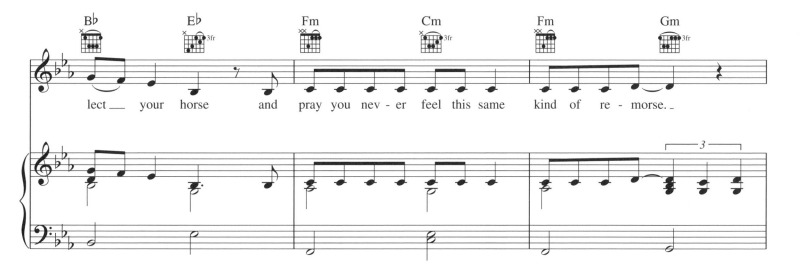

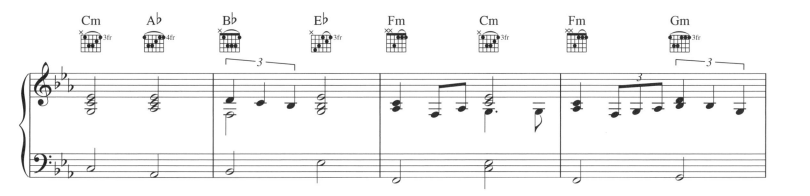

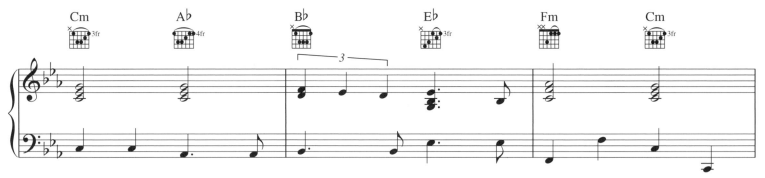

Seal my heart and break __ my pride. I've

Instrumental

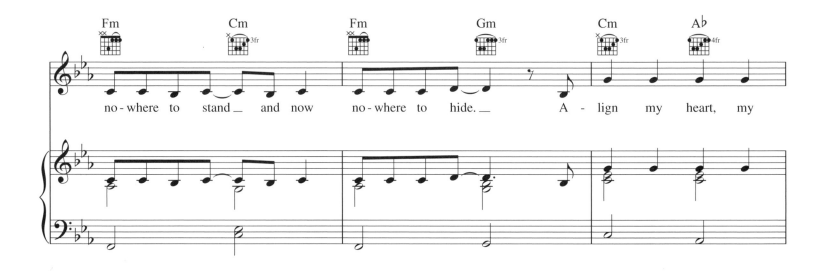

no- where to stand __ and now no- where to hide. __ A - lign my heart, my

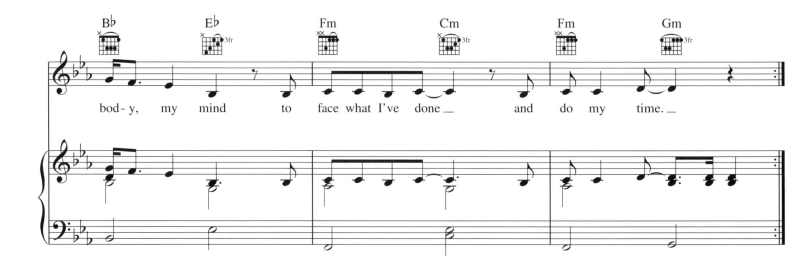

bod- y, my mind to face what I've done __ and do my time. __

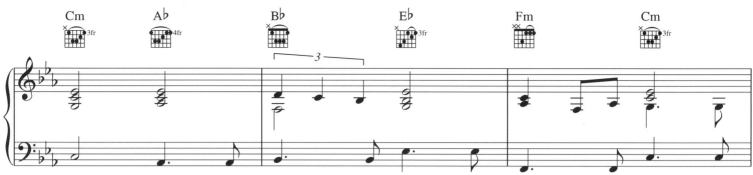

Seal my heart and break _ my pride. I've

no - where to stand _ and now no - where to hide. _ A - lign my heart, my

bod - y, my mind to face what I've done _ and do my time. _

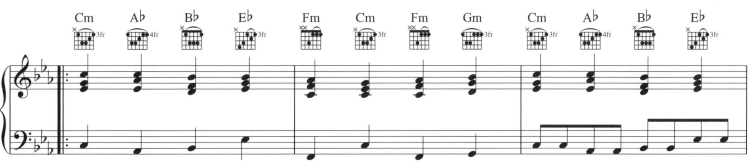

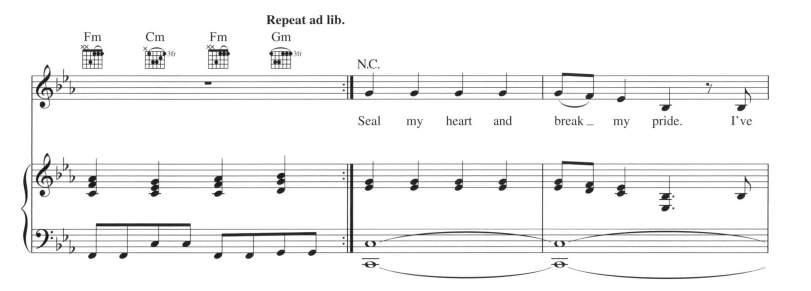

Repeat ad lib.

Seal my heart and break _ my pride. I've

no-where to stand _ and now no-where to hide. _ A - lign my heart, my

Drums

bod-y, my mind to face what I've done _ and do my time. _

Play 4 times ad lib.

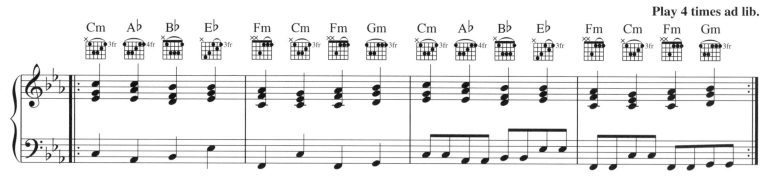

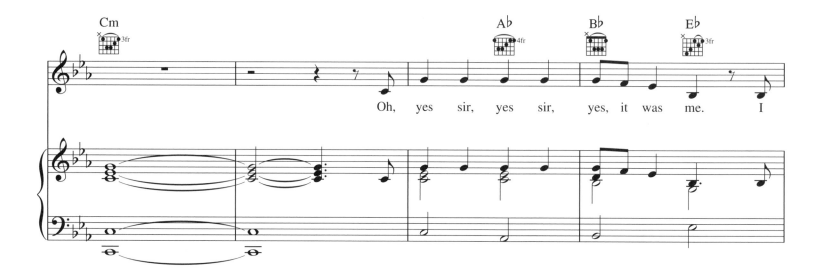

Oh, yes sir, yes sir, yes, it was me. I

know what I've done, _ 'cause I know what I've seen. _ I went out back and I

got _ my gun. I said, "You have-n't met _ me, I am the on-ly son."

AFTER THE STORM

Words and Music by
MUMFORD & SONS

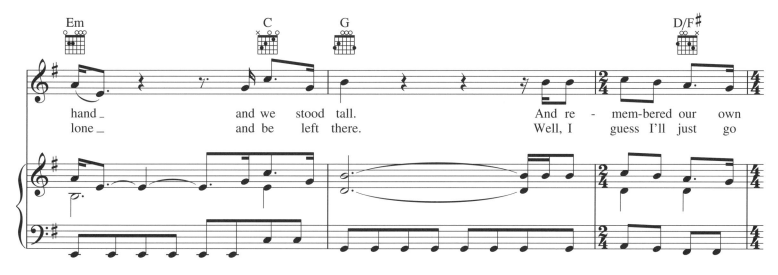

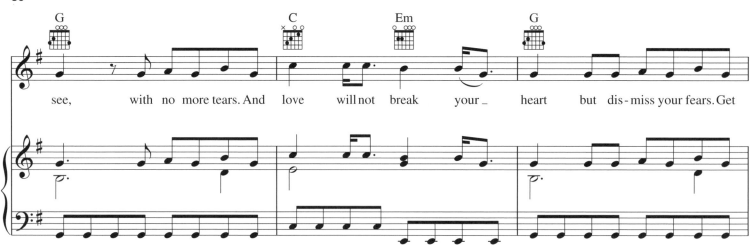

see, with no more tears. And love will not break your _ heart but dis-miss your fears. Get

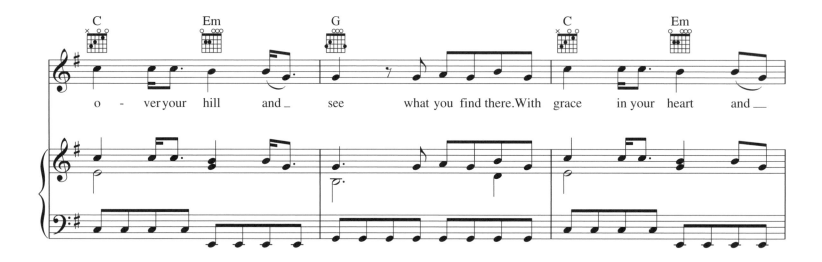

o - ver your hill and _ see what you find there. With grace in your heart and _

flow - ers in your hair. _

D.S. al Coda

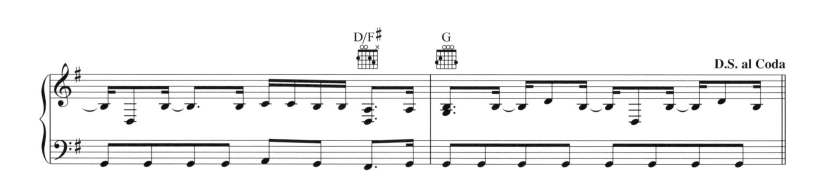

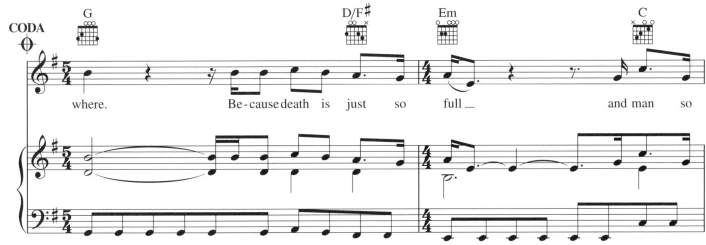

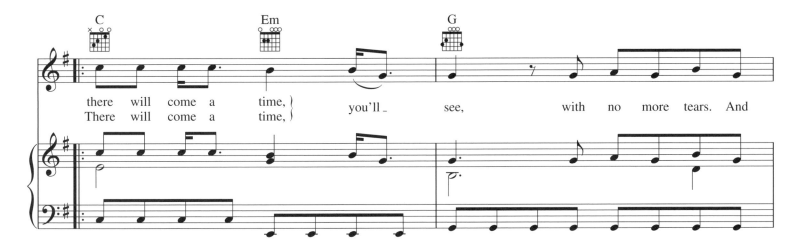

CODA

where. Be-cause death is just so full ___ and man so

small. Well, I'm scared of what's be - hind ___ and what's be -

fore. But

there will come a time, } you'll ___ see, with no more tears. And
There will come a time, }

love will not break your heart but dis-miss your fears. Get o - ver your hill and

see what you find there. With grace in your heart and flow - ers in your hair.

flow - ers in your hair.